Espionage's
Most Wanted

Espionage's Most Wanted

The Top 10 Book of Malicious
Moles, Blown Covers, and
Intelligence Oddities

Tom E. Mahl

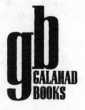

GALAHAD
BOOKS

First Galahad Books edition pubished in 2006.

Galahad Books
A division of BBS Publishing Corporation
450 Raritan Center Parkway
Edison, New Jersey 08837

Galahad Books is a registered trademark of BBS Publishing Corporation.

Published by arrangement with Potomac Books, Inc.

Most Wanted ® is a registered trade mark of Potomac Books, Inc. and is used under license.

Distributed by Sterling Publishing Company, Inc.
387 Park Avenue South, New York, NY 10016

Distributed in Canada by Sterling Publishing c/o Canadian Manda Group
165 Dufferin Street, Toronto, Ontario, Canada M6K 3H6

Distributed in Great Britain by Chrysalis Book Group PLC
The Chrysalis Building Bromley Road, London W106SP England

Distributed in Australia by Capricorn Link (Australia) Pty, Ltd.
PO Box 704, Windsor NSW 2756 Australia

For information about special sales, premium and corporate purchases, please
contact Sterling Special Sales Department at 800-805-5489 or
specialsales@sterlingpub.com

Library of Congress Catalog Card number: 2002156001

ISBN 10: 1-57866-158-7
ISBN 13: 978-1-57866-158-9
Printed in the United States of America.

This book is dedicated to my daughter
Tracy Renee Mahl

Contents

Photographs

Acknowledgments

For their cheerful helpfulness despite my endless tedious questions, I would like to thank the reference librarians at Lorain County Community College Library: Rita Blanford, Helen DeBalzo, Denise Karshner, Betty Kunes, Susan Paul, Christine Sheetz, Ann Marie Smeraldi, Michael Stein, and Sarah Wharton. Thanks also to the staff of the Case Western Reserve Library, and to the National Security Agency for its cooperation in providing photographs. For their thoughts and suggestions my deep appreciation goes out to Vincent McHale, Hayden Peake, and Yvonne Scarbrough. And, finally, for the run of his library of intelligence books as well as several photographs, thanks also to the late Fred Lewton of the Northern Ohio Chapter of the Association of Former Intelligence Officers. I, of course, take responsibility for all errors and problems in the text.

Introduction

The world of spies and espionage has a long and interesting, if not well-known, history. From the Bible, to the records of George Washington in the American Revolution, to the newspapers of today every age has had its espionage triumphs and failures. In the Old Testament Moses sent Joshua to spy out the land of Canaan. (Note Moses' excellent tradecraft: Joshua was a cover name for Hosea, son of Noon.) With this experience and eager for conquest, Joshua later sent his spies to Jericho where Rahab the Harlot successfully hid them on the roof of her brothel. Thus Joshua, 2:6, gives us one of the first of many references connecting harlots to espionage.

George Washington is well known as the father of our country but less renowned as a founder of American spying. Bitter, nearly fatal, experience had impressed upon him the importance of intelligence during the Seven Years' War (1756–1763), where for lack of inside information he found himself part of an ambushed army. For his ignorance, he had two horses shot from under him and four bullet holes in his clothes. Washington's commander in this battle did even less well, having lost five horses and his life. Lack of intelligence information could indeed be costly. Some of Washington's Revolutionary War (1775–1783) spy ventures turned out well; the Culper Ring, which reported to George Washington from British-occupied Manhattan, comes to mind. On the other hand, Nathan Hale, sent earlier to spy out Manhattan, had ended as the center of attention at a hanging party.

Not that G. W. was alone; the Second Continental Congress set up its own Committee of Secret Correspondence to gather intelligence information. The most famous members—Benjamin Franklin, John Jay, and John Dickinson—directed secret agents not only in the colonies but also in London and Paris, doing all the things good spies do. No matter what modern moralists might suggest, the founding fathers were not, as you will see, simple backcountry innocents when it came to espionage (or a lot of other things, for that matter).

This book is meant for the entertainment and enlightenment of the general reader, but there are also printed here a number of items heretofore known only to a few intelligence officers and buried in secret government files.

In addition, a small related *caveat* is in order here. In reading thousands of pages of espionage books, I have frequently been taken aback by the errors that creep into the work of even the best scholars in this field. There are at least two major causes of these problems. First, often these facts are nicely footnoted and cited, but—alas—intelligence officers only repeat the errors of others until these mistakes have been sort of grandfathered into the lore as gospel.

Second, the definitive facts of many of these events often remain classified and buried in the archives of the intelligence agencies for decades after the agency has discovered the truth. The public and public writers are left to speculate.

An example is the case of John Cairncross, the so-called Fifth Man of a group of Soviet agents who penetrated British Intelligence and the Foreign Office in the 1930s, '40s and '50s. To write this, I have walked from my office in Mather House (a woman's dorm in Cairncross's day) over to the Mather Memorial building, where Cairncross had his office at Case Western Reserve University (Western Reserve University then). I have thought this only fitting because one of the great spies of the twentieth century was, in 1964, the head of the romance language department then housed there. As I went over his FBI file it struck me that we must know much less about this man than we think we do. Most of his FBI file as reviewed by the FBI in 1998 and 1999 remains secret (see sample pages in photo section) almost forty years after the FBI knew him to be a Soviet spy and four years after his death.

Two striking things are revealed, however: Contrary to much of the published work on Cairncross (alas, including my own previous work), the FBI knew he had been a Soviet agent before he arrived in Cleveland in February 1964 and, thus, he felt comfortable volunteering to work for the FBI as a double agent against the Soviets. If even ten percent of the withheld material is of such bombshell caliber, then this file would completely change our understanding of Cairncross and what he did. This also makes one wonder about our public knowledge of Cairncross's friends Burgess, Philby, Maclean, and Blunt, who also penetrated the high reaches of British Intelligence for Soviet Intelligence.

The great days of twentieth-century espionage history are ahead of, not behind, us. So my effort here is to make the following stories as complete as possible at this time. Insiders are welcome to comment.

The modern era of espionage—covert action, code breaking, plausible denials, assassinations, planted lovers, propaganda, and assorted, often colorful, dirty tricks—begins just before World War I with the British creation of two, then very secret, organizations. Military Intelligence 5 (MI-5), created in 1909, was for domestic work, much like the American FBI. Military Intelligence 6 (MI-6), created in 1911, was akin to the CIA. One ex-MI-5 agent, Peter Wright, later summed up this wonderful work in his memoir, *Spycatcher:* "We bugged and burgled our way across London at the State's behest, while pompous bowler-hatted civil servants in Whitehall pretended to look the other way."

So step now into the secret world so often unacknowledged by both government officials and standard history books.

By Their Names You Will Not Know Them

A ll intelligence agencies love code names and cover symbols. Here are some of my favorites.

1. ACID GAMBIT

In the late 1980s a CIA agent named Kurt Muse was caught in Panama while setting up a "black" radio station in Panama City. The purpose of the station was to broadcast anti-Manuel Noriega propaganda for which the United States would not appear responsible. Acid Gambit was the name of the operation to rescue the hapless Muse from his captors. After numerous rehearsals, the U.S. Army's elite Delta Force rescued him from the *Comandancia* without a hitch. Unfortunately, his helicopter crashed shortly thereafter and another chopper had to rescue him a second time.

2. MINCEMEAT

The British are good at these scam operations. Operation Mincemeat was part of the Barclay deception plan, a ruse designed to ease the path for the Allied invasion of Sicily in 1943. Mincemeat was the code name for the operation to create "The Man Who Never Was," Major

1

William Martin, Royal Marines. None of these decep-
tions would have been as effective or as attractive had
not the Brits been reading the German Enigma Ciphers,
which gave a constant backcheck on how the Germans
were taking the bait. In Operation Mincemeat, the British took the corpse of a man who had died of natural
causes and kept it frozen while concocting a phony history and personal life for him—love letters, a receipt
for an engagement ring, a notice from his bank of an
overdraft, a letter from his father telling him to meet the
family solicitor to discuss money matters, even theater
ticket stubs. They dressed him in a major's uniform and
attached an attaché case full of phony documents saying the Allies' Mediterranean attack would take place
in Greece or Sardinia. Major Martin's body was then
dumped out of a submarine off Spain to wash ashore.
The Spanish turned copies over to their German friends
and the deception was on.

3. **BRIDE**

This was the American effort in the 1940s to read the
Soviet coded messages sent between New York and
Moscow Center. The messages were supposed to be
unbreakable because they used onetime pads of random numbers. However, under wartime conditions, the
Soviets had a shortage of printed sheets and duplicated
some of the pages. A clever American found a way to
spot those messages from the multiple-use pads. The
Americans may also have acquired part of a Soviet
code book. At any rate, this very secret project enabled
the United States to discover a large number of Soviet
agents, collaborators, and contacts in the White House,
the OSS, the State Department, the Treasury, and the
Manhattan Project. This information largely confirmed

the accusations of ex-Communist agents Elizabeth Bentley and Whittaker Chambers. It was hard to go into court with this information because the code breaking was thought much more important than prosecuting individual Soviet agents. It was not until the 1990s that this project, under another randomly chosen, meaningless code name, "Venona," became public knowledge. Coupled with material from the Communist Party archives we now have firm evidence that the Soviets had some 350 agents, collaborators, and informants in the U.S. government during the Stalin era.

4. **SCANATE, GRILL FLAME, CENTER LANE, STARGATE, SUNSTREAK**

All these are cover names for the CIA's effort to use a team of psychics to "remotely view" places of interest, particularly Soviet places of interest. This project, dating from the early 1980s into the 1990s, is said to have been housed at Fort George Meade, Maryland.

5. **MURRAY HILL AREA, COMBINED DEVELOPMENT TRUST, GENERAL DEVELOPMENT TRUST**

These were various names for part of the Manhattan Project, the secret effort to build an atomic bomb. The Combined Development Trust et al. attempted to gain a monopoly on the world supply of uranium to keep it from the Germans and later from the Soviets. The major activity of this project was buying the rights to ores mined in the Belgian Congo, in Africa. This project failed for two simple reasons: First, unknown to the West, the Russians had their own vast reserves of uranium; second, it flew in the face of the laws of supply and demand. The worldwide purchases drove up the price of uranium, thus signaling to prospectors that they could become rich by finding new deposits, which they did. Defeating the laws of supply and demand is tough work.

6. JEHHIFER

This was a CIA project to raise a Soviet submarine, the K-129, which had blown up in April 1968 and sunk in 17,000 feet of water in the Pacific Ocean. The American hydrophone system, "Sea Spider," detected the accident and gave the CIA the location. Given the go-ahead by National Security Advisor Henry Kissinger, the CIA built a special ship, the *Glomar Explorer,* to do the work. The cover story was that secretive business-man Howard Hughes built the ship for an undersea mining project. In the summer of 1974, a large me-chanical claw grabbed the sub. When the story broke in February 1975 the published reports said only half of the sub had been retrieved and that we did not get the codebooks, only some nuclear torpedoes and eight bodies of Soviet sailors. The sailors were buried at sea with full military honors. How much of the published story is correct was and is an open question.

7. LACE

The Berlin Wall fell in the autumn of 1989, but it was not until early in 1990 that a mob of 20,000 people stormed the headquarters of the East German Ministry of State Security, popularly known as the Stasi. The Stasi had intruded into every aspect of life and its peo-ple had been diligently burning files, but their task was so immense that when the mob showed up 180,000 meters of files remained. Among the unburned were documents showing that every American agent in that country had been blown. Lace was the joint CIA/FBI operation to discover the mole in American intelli-gence. Lace failed to find the culprit, as did Playactor and skylight. But the CIA and FBI kept at it and finally got their man—Aldrich Ames.

8. ULTRA

This is the name of both the effort to break the German Enigma cipher and the resulting readable messages. Though the British effort began in 1938, the real breakthrough came in the summer of 1939 when the Polish gave the British copies of the German Enigma machines and the results of their groundbreaking research. This British effort was based at Bletchley Park, a large English estate. Here, with the aid of a primitive computer, a "Bombe," analysts began to read the German messages in April 1940. As their skill increased the British were able to read German orders just as quickly as the German addressees. Though 25,000 people knew about this code breaking it was kept secret from both the Germans and the public. Not until the 1970s did anything appear in English about this program. The Soviets, of course knew about it very early. For one thing, Soviet spy John Cairncross worked at Bletchley Park.

9. GOLD

Perhaps it would be apropos to say that what appeared to be gold ended no better than bronze. Gold was a mid-1950s CIA/MI-6 project to build a tunnel 1,500 feet into the Soviet sector of Berlin to tap the communication cables running from Berlin to Moscow. If nothing else, the tunnel was a first-class project whose builders obviously thought of it as a long-term project. It had all the amenities. The U.S. Corp of Engineers built the tunnel 15 or 20 feet deep, with a reinforced concrete floor and walls, electricity, and a ventilation system. The best electronic equipment was installed in the eastern interception chamber where CIA technicians could carefully tap the exposed cables at their leisure. There was a delicious flow of information, conversations between the East German government and Moscow, the Soviet Embassy in Berlin and Berlin and Soviet Army Headquarters in Moscow.

In addition to the conversations there were elaborately coded messages, deemed unbreakable. Happily these did not need to be attacked. There was a ghost signal, from the keyboarding of the original plaintext, riding the cable with the coded message. Enhanced, it could be run out on a teleprinter in plaintext. This happy state of affairs might have gone on for a long time except that George Blake, a Soviet spy in Britain's MI-6, was stationed in Berlin. He blew the whistle on the tunnel. The Soviets allowed it to operate until the spring of 1956 when they made an elaborate show of accidentally discovering the tunnel and its communications chamber. To what extent the Russians realized that their impenetrable cipher system had been breached is hard to know.

10.   OPERATION POPEYE

This was the weather modification program conducted by the United States over North Vietnam. In an example of the law of unintended consequences, Popeye is thought to be the cause of the failure of Operation Ivory Coast, the mission to rescue American prisoners held by the North at Sontay, North Vietnam. The helicopter-borne assault went without a hitch but found no prisoners. They had been moved because of the rising floodwaters of the nearby Red River, which had been caused by Popeye.

By Their names you Are not Supposed to Know Them

E very profession has its arcane language, its jargon, that makes it easier for the chosen few to communicate and difficult for others to know what they are talking about. Here are some of my favorite spookspeak terms.

1. SHEEP-DIPPED

This is the practice of officially dropping people or equipment from the United States military or intelligence agency payrolls, only to have them employed at the same job by a civilian company or even a foreign entity. For example, during the Vietnam War the United States built a secret radar installation, "Heavy Green," on a remote mountain in a neighboring neutral country, Laos. The purpose was to help direct the "Rolling Thunder" bombing campaign of North Vietnam. The military personnel running "Heavy Green" were dropped from the military rolls and ostensibly took civilian jobs with Lockheed Aircraft. The Communists found "Rolling Thunder" quite annoying and they destroyed "Heavy Green" after only a few months. The U.S. Air Force completed the job by napalming the site to obliterate any evidence that the United States had based a military site in a neutral country. They never did recover all the bodies. The U.S. military tried similar tactics prior to Vietnam. Before the Japanese bombed Pear Harbor, President Roosevelt and his advisers were doing their best to aggravate the Japanese military in China. Members of the U.S. Army Air Force were dropped from the rolls and "volunteered" for the Chinese Air Force. The United States also supplied the planes and the money so that these flyers could fight the Japanese in China. There was even a plan to have these flyers supplied with bombers so that they could bomb Tokyo. Of course, we would have known nothing about this had it happened and the Japanese protested. The U.S. government denied these were U.S. pilots until about a decade ago when it finally admitted that the Flying Tigers were U.S. military personnel, entitled to their veterans' benefits and medals.

2. BLACK BAG JOB

This is an FBI term for an illegal, warrantless entry by a specially trained team with the goal of photographing documents, planting bugs, or stealing. It usually takes a minimum of eight people to do this sort of job properly. The FBI did hundreds of these jobs under J. Edgar Hoover, ranging from embassies to the dwellings of antiwar radicals and Ku Klux Klan wizards. Some of the people thus trained found their way to the Nixon White House "Plumbers" group set up to stop the leaks that had bedeviled the president. A teaching colleague of mine once asked G. Gordon Liddy "How in the hell did you guys get caught [at Watergate]? You were pros." Liddy replied: " I don't know. It went okay in practice."

3. **DANGLE**

This is a standard ploy in the great game of espionage. A prospective spy or defector is "dangled" by one intelligence service in front of a hostile intelligence service like a worm in front of a fish. The purported spy or defector will put on an elaborate ruse to feed disinformation to the other side. Intelligence agencies are very alert to this gambit, and intelligence annals are full of woeful tales of sincere traitors, with real secret documents in hand, being thrown out of embassies.

4. **DRY CLEANING**

These are tactics used by a subject to shake off those tailing him or her or to establish whether he or she is actually being tailed. Standard tactics are getting onto a subway car, walking right through and out the other door just before the doors close; walking a twisting course through the city punctuated by taking cabs for a few turning blocks; and going into buildings and using the elevators in a similar manner.

5. **MOONLIGHT EXTRADITION**

This is extradition without all that inconvenient paperwork and all those time-consuming hearings that so bog down a real, legal extradition. The authorities of a friendly state deliver the accused to the border—no questions asked—as a gesture of fraternal solidarity with their fellow law officers in another country. Example: On January 25, 1993, a Pakistani, Mir Aimal Kansi, shot and killed two CIA men and wounded three others with an AK-47 as they sat in a line of cars waiting to enter the Agency headquarters at Langley, Virginia. He then fled to Afghanistan. Four and a half years and a two-million-dollar reward later, certain "Afghan individuals" delivered Kansi to the Pakistani border where he was put on a plane and flown to the United States.

6. GRINDER

A "grinder" is a safe house used for debriefing enemy defectors. American intelligence and counterintelligence have dozens of these places convenient to Washington, D.C. Here the defector is fed and sheltered in seclusion. If done properly he will not know where he is as he goes over and over his story in a process that may take months. One very nice safe house is in the 800 block of Canal Drive in Great Falls, Virginia. This is where Soviet defector Anatoli Golitsyn spun out his mole-in-every-U.S. agency tales that CIA's counterintelligence chief James Angleton found so compelling. There might as well have been a mole. Angleton and Golytsyn never did find one, but many say the hunt for a mole did as much damage as several moles could have accomplished.

7. FALSE FLAG

Recruiting agents with the false belief that they are really helping some organization that shares their beliefs or seems innocent enough is a false flag tactic. Example: When in 1940 British Intelligence agent Elizabeth Thorpe Pack seduced Charles Brousse, an attaché at the Vichy French Embassy in Washington, she flew a false flag. She told him that she was working for the Americans because Brousse had a lot of bad feeling for the British. The Brits had killed a thousand French sailors to keep the French fleet from falling into German hands after the French had surrendered to the Germans in June 1940. (Churchill also did this to prove to the Americans how serious the British were about pursuing the war.) Another example: Markus Wolf, the head of the communist East German foreign intelligence service, reported this recruitment of a woman agent within NATO by one of his Romeo spies: "They spent their first night together and the next morning he emptied his heart to her—some of it anyway. He told his new love that he was an officer with Danish military intelligence, explaining that the small nations like Denmark often felt left out in NATO and needed their own confidential information." It worked; she was hooked and landed.

8. **WEEDER**

A weeder is an intelligence officer charged with deleting material from intelligence documents before they are sent to open archives. Weeders generally err on the side of caution—large amounts of material from World War II, for instance, are still withheld. But weeders being human beings, and intelligence being so compartmentalized, few have the perfect knowledge always to recognize the importance of what they are reading. Thus, the researcher with a durable keister may be able to find the overlooked gems he needs, but this is hard-rock mining with hand tools. A British historian used the word well in his nice review of my first book, *Desperate Deception: British Covert Operations in the United States, 1939–44*: "Tom Mahl has written the book that a generation of document weeders on both sides of the Atlantic worked to try to ensure would never see print."

9. "DEVISED," ANOTHER WORD FOR PHONY

In the heyday of the CIA's cultural wars against the Soviets, the Agency passed millions of dollars through foundations to such groups as the National Student Association and the Congress for Cultural Freedom. In the mid-1970s the U.S. Senate investigated these operations and wrote: "Most of the funds were transmitted through legitimate or "devised" foundations—that is, fictitious entities established by the CIA." A first-class example was the dummy Fairfield Foundation originally set up to finance the Masterpieces of the Twentieth Century festival in Paris in 1952. It was continued because it was so useful and its board was so compliant. The "president" and resident sugar daddy of the Fairfield Foundation could not have been more out of place; he was the tightwad multimillionaire Julius Fleischmann of yeast and gin fame. Fleischmann loved masquerading as a sensitive philanthropist while giving away piles of other people's money.

The Fairfield's board of directors met solemnly every other month and faithfully approved all the prearranged payments—just as solemnly as if they had been making real decisions. There would often be a guest from the Congress for Cultural Freedom, often someone close to the CIA or MI-6. The board members who participated in CIA and MI-6 projects included: Cass Canfield, a close friend of CIA director Allen Dulles; Frank Platt, a CIA man; Gardner "Mike" Cowles head of Cowles, media empire and a longtime participant in projects run by British and American intelligence; Joseph Verner Reid, president of the Hobe Sound Company of Florida, where upper intelligence people vacationed together; Whitelaw Reid of the ownership family of the *New York Herald Tribune*, which had been used so well by British Intelligence during World War II. John Thompson, a CIA man, served as executive director.

10. SOFT FILES

These are the nitty-gritty files that all intelligence agencies, including the State Department and its embassies, compile on everyone important to them, even their dear friends in journalism. Here we find the good stuff: drinking habits, sex habits, money problems, odd interests, and odd friends. Being unofficial, unregistered, and most useful they are unlikely to be given up to nosy outsiders like courts of law, congressional investigating committees, or even the White House. Presidents, congressmen and judges come and go, but the soft files stay put.

Ten Tools of the Trade

H ere we will just touch the surface of the toys the boys and girls of the espionage trade get to play with. If your interest is piqued by this small sampling, get a copy of *The Ultimate Spy Book* by H. Keith Melton. This fine volume has some 600 illustrations of the gizmos that make the spy's work a little easier.

1. GETTING IN

Here (p. 15) is the handy little tool kit an expert would use to gain entry to an office or any door protected by a pin tumbler lock. If you know how to use these little picks, tension wrenches, and rakes, you are undoubtedly an expert—or reading this in a cell somewhere.

2. AUTOMATED GETTING IN

One constant in capitalist society is the search for ways to eliminate the need for expensive skilled labor. Espionage is no exception. You really have to know what you are doing and maybe have some talent with a lock-picking kit, but there are also little electronic devices that do most of the work for you. Insert the tool, switch it on, and *voila*.

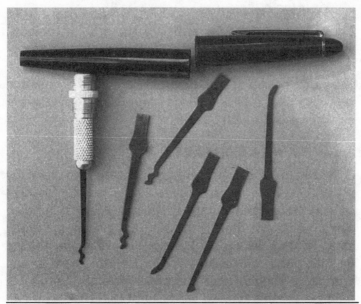

This nice lock-picking kit is hidden in a pen. On the left are the rakes. On the right are three feeler picks. The clip on the pen is used as a tension wrench.

3. GETTING OUT

Well—getting in went okay, but you got caught, à la the Watergate burglars. Maybe the prisons in the country of your confinement are not very pretty. (Let me assure you, gentle reader, that no matter what the talk shows say about "country club prisons," you would not want to spend your time in even the nicest prisons.) A little kit of reamers, drills, and saws in a handy, concealable case (that can be hidden in the rectum) is just what the breakout artist needs. The CIA supplied this particular kit in the 1960s. And you always wondered what those orifice checks were all about.

4. ORIFICE CHECK II

Those who wish to be armed without being obvious should check out this little KGB single-shot rectal pistol. Just hold the knurled ring and twist the barrel. If you had enough space, it would be sort of a matched set with the tool kit. As I have said elsewhere—espionage is a tough business.

5. WHAT THE KIDON CARRY

Undoubtedly the most practiced assassins presently plying the trade are members of the Israeli Mossad's assassination teams, called "Kidon." Admittedly, they use a variety of tools, including explosives, gas, and guns—but the handgun of choice is a .22-caliber Italian Beretta pistol with silencer. The Beretta is small and compact, rugged and reliable—certainly admirable features for this type of work. I am told that "you can swish it around in a bucket of mud or in the sand and come out shooting." When equipped with a silencer (works just like the muffler on your car) and loaded with subsonic rounds (the bullet breaking the sound barrier is what makes the loud crack), it makes little more noise than a BB gun. While perfect for those with smaller hands, those with larger mitts often complain about the hammer biting into their hands. Oh well, you will probably be wearing gloves. Those who took part in killing 11 Israelis at the 1972 Olympics were tracked down by the Kidon. Those who were shot took a commemorative 11 rounds from this little beauty.

6. MADE IN AMERICA

During World War II the OSS research and development branch built a very fine, silenced .22-caliber pistol using the American-made Hi-Standard pistol. With its

OSS silencer, you could still use the sights, there was no muzzle flash, and it was very quiet. The word is that Bill Donovan, head of the OSS, was so impressed with this fine tool that he took it and a couple of sandbags over to the White House and gave President Roosevelt a demo. The purpose of such an instrument in the American arsenal is said, of course, to be utterly benign. It is to "allow downed pilots and agents behind enemy lines to hunt small game without being detected." It was U-2 pilot Francis Gary Powers who had a Hi-Standard model HD-MS with silencer on him when captured in the Soviet Union. The Russians still have this pistol on display in Moscow. Those in the trade call this the "Powers Model" in his memory. My experienced friends tell me that in a pinch you can make a silencer that works just as well by. . . .

7. NO HOLES

The problem with both of the above pistols is that no matter how well you use them an autopsy leaves little doubt about why the victim quit breathing. This is fine if you do not care or if you wish to send a signal, but in many covert operations you would rather that the death be unattributable, chalked up to an accident or a quirk of nature. You have the victim out of your hair and there is none of this eye-for-an-eye stuff that can turn into a free-for-all or run out of control like the 1914 assassination of Archduke Franz Ferdinand and his wife that brought on World War I and turned the world upside down.

To this end, the Soviet intelligence services and their Eastern Bloc helpers spent much time and thought perfecting the gas gun, whose results baffled the autopsy experts. The killer here was a KGB officer named Bogdan Stashinsky. The victims were two

Ukrainian dissidents living in West Germany, Lev Rebet in 1957 and Stefan Bandera in 1959. For this work, Stashinsky received the Order of the Red Banner. When Stashinsky pressed the lever on this seven-inch gas gun, which he had wrapped in a newspaper, it released a firing pin, detonating a cap. This small explosion broke an ampule of cyanide, vaporizing it. The vapor spewed forth from a hole carefully screened to prevent glass shards in the face of the victims. Stashinsky caught both Rebet and Bandera in darkened stairwells—only a couple of feet away. The authorities thought Rebet had suffered a heart attack, but they caught on to the cause of Bandera's death.

Despite all the accolades back at KGB headquarters, Stashinsky had become involved with a German woman who was against this sort of thing. They defected in 1961 and Stashinsky confessed to the West German police. He was tried and given a light sentence of eight years. The bad publicity generated by the trial convinced the Soviet authorities to put away assassination as an everyday tool and use it only on special occasions. The 1979 killing of President Hafizullah Amin of Afghanistan is cited by historians as being one of those occasions.

8. THE BULGARIAN UMBRELLA TRICK

Though the KGB no longer dirtied its hands by killing every talkative dissident it could find, the Eastern bloc countries still needed such services—enter the Bulgarians. The émigré Bulgarian writer Georgi Markov, who worked for the BBC World Service Bulgarian section, was making himself a nuisance attacking the Bulgarian Communist government. Therefore, as a sign of Communist solidarity the KGB supplied the Bulgarians with a special umbrella. In 1978 Markov was jabbed with

National Security Agency

In 1946, Soviet school children presented this replica of the great
seal of the United States to Ambassador Averell Harriman. The
ambassador hung this seal in his office in Spasso House, his official
residence. During George F. Kennan's ambassadorship in 1952, a
routine security check discovered that the seal contained a
wireless, battery-less microphone.

this bumbershoot near Waterloo Bridge in London. It
injected a small hollow pellet into his thigh. The pellet
contained ricin, a highly toxic poison made from the
castor bean. Although he lived long enough to tell of
the stranger who had poked him, the doctors could not
find the pellet, and he died. Scarcely a week later in
Paris another Bulgarian émigré, Vladimir Kostov, got
the same treatment, but the doctors located and extracted the pellet before much of the ricin could escape.
He lived.

The bugged seal's resonant cavity and microphone. Sound waves
amplified by the hollow, resonant cavity made the
microphone's tail vibrate. These vibrations were picked up
by radio waves beamed from outside the residence and
converted back into sound waves.

q. CANDY IS DANDY BUT BOMBS WILL . . .

A 1994 book titled *Special Tasks: The Memoirs of an
Unwanted Witness—A Soviet Spymaster* by Pavel Sudoplatov and Anatoli Sudoplatov, with Jerrold L. and
Leona P. Schecter, tells many tales of Pavel's work.
One "special task," assigned him personally by Stalin
was to assassinate the troublesome Ukrainian national-
ist leader Yevhen Konovalets. Sudoplatov gave Konovalets a box of his favorite bonbons. Unfortunately, the
bonbons contained a bomb, which killed the Ukrainian
leader.

10. **ALL THE WORLD LOVES A GREAT LISTENER—OR MAYBE NOT**

Once upon a time, the generous Soviets gave the U.S. ambassador in Moscow a wonderful gift—a wooden carving of the Great Seal of the United States. One fine September day in 1952, electronics experts were sweeping Spasso House, the American Embassy, for bugs. They found nothing. On a brainstorm or a whim one of the technicians asked ambassador George Kennan to start talking as if he were dictating a letter. Soon the technician returned and, motioning to Kennan to keep it up, "he removed the seal [from the wall], took up a mason's hammer, and began to hack to pieces the brick wall where the seal had been . . . [then] he turned these destructive attentions on the seal itself." Although it was clear that the device he found was sending out every golden word the ambassador spoke, it took a long time to figure out how the battery-less, circuit-less device worked. Nicknamed "The Thing," it was beyond the state of western electronic art.

Eventually British MI-5 officer Peter Wright (author of *Spycatcher*) discovered that the hollow metal device with the spike tail was a "cavity resonator." Voice vibrations started the cylindrical metal device vibrating. The Soviets bounced microwaves off the tuning-fork-like tail and converted the reflection back into sound waves; every word the ambassador spoke went into the Soviet record. The Brits were so impressed that they created a copy of "The Thing," called it Satyr, and even supplied them to the Americans.

The Elite

There have been a number of intelligence agencies, considered the best of the twentieth century, that have had such influence on others that they should be mentioned here. Some are well known and others you may never have heard of.

1. THE BOLSHOI INTELLIGENCE AGENCY

Bolshoi means *big* in Russian, and at its peak before the fall of the Soviet Union in 1991, the usual estimates were that the Committee for State Security, the KGB, had 1.2 million employees. They bent to the tasks performed by several agencies in most countries—everything from guarding the borders to seducing foreign embassy personnel to creating some of the most sophisticated bugging and surveillance devices known to man. Until the early 1990s, the KGB was a combination CIA, FBI, NSA, Border Patrol, Secret Service, and postal inspection service.

2. THE PUZZLE PALACE

James Bamford's fine book by this title (*The Puzzle Palace*) is the best on the subject of the National Security

Agency (NSA). This mammoth agency is headquartered at Fort George G. Meade, Maryland. NSA has over 120,000 employees, making it six times larger than the Central Intelligence Agency. These are the people responsible for intercepting the communications of foreign countries and breaking their coded messages. The NSA is also responsible for making secure codes and ciphers for the U.S. government.

NSA was created in 1952 to bring together all the scattered cryptology services of the various military services, then working in isolation from one another. Any signal that goes up into the air is fair game for these people as their giant computers search conversations for key words that will start the recording machines. Its efficiency is startling. Remember President Reagan playing the tapes of the Soviet pilots' conversations while shooting down flight 007 as it crossed into Soviet airspace? To grab a particular set of conversations from the thousands taking place at any one time was certainly a technical *tour de force*.

I am not sure the NSA appreciated the president's public display of their talents, however. Until 20 years or so ago NSA was a super-secret outfit, whose name rarely appeared in public print.

3. THE AGENCY, THE COMPANY, BY ANY OTHER NAME THE CENTRAL INTELLIGENCE AGENCY

Bill Donovan's Office of Strategic Services was disbanded after the war because President Harry Truman said he did not want a spy agency. This noble thought did not last long, as the world's greatest power was not able to slip back off center stage after World War II. On January 24, 1946, Truman invited Rear Admiral William H. Sours to lunch. Sours was the first head of the

CIA's immediate predecessor, the Central Intelligence Group. Truman invested Sours as "chief spook" and gave him the instruments of the office—a black cloak and a wooden dagger. The CIA is certainly the best known of the world's intelligence agencies. No others have been put through the public examination that the CIA suffered at the hands of congressional committees during the mid-1970s. Often publicly vilified, the Agency has seemed to gain new life and respect since September 11, 2001, when the United States was attacked by terrorists. Many of the sillier criticisms of the Agency have disappeared from the public dialogue.

4. AMERICAN COUNTERINTELLIGENCE, THE FBI

J. Edgar Hoover is long gone, but the Bureau he set in motion is still functioning. As the nation's main counterintelligence agency, the Federal Bureau of Investigation (FBI) is the outfit in charge of catching spies and other criminals in the United States. Be aware that in spite of textbook definitions restricting it to within the borders of the United States, the FBI does operate in foreign countries, lots of them. Going well back to Hoover's days, the FBI has stationed "legal attachés" in foreign countries, particularly in Latin America.

Yes, the ordinary garden variety tails follow the KGB and GRU agent around Washington and New York in cheap, government-issue Plymouth sedans in bland colors. The pair of guys in white shirts and ties in the Plymouth are just starters, though. Backing them up or even leading the way are members of the FBI's Special Support Group (SSG) or "Gs" to those in the trade. They are ordinary-looking students, housewives, and even retired people who anonymously tail subjects of the Bureau's choosing for about one-third the pay of an FBI special agent.

5. GRU TO YOU

The GRU is the Chief Intelligence Directorate of the General Staff of the Red Army. It was created by Leon Trotsky during the Russian Civil War that followed the Communist Revolution of 1917. This may be somewhat misleading—the GRU has much wider duties and interests than we might associate with strictly military matters. Technically, the GRU is subordinate to the KGB. The Soviet spy ring exposed after World War II by a code clerk who defected in Canada was a GRU ring. Much of the heavy lifting needed to steal the secrets of the Manhattan Project was done by the GRU. Richard Sorge, the Soviet super spy in Japan during World War II, was another GRU agent. There have been some problems, also. Oleg Penkovsky was a GRU man. The material he gave Britain and the United States on Soviet developments in rockets allowed Kennedy to call Khrushchev's bluff in the Cuban Missile Crisis of 1962. Kennedy knew that the Soviets did not have the missiles for a nuclear exchange.

6. DAS MINISTERIUM FUR STAATSSICHERHEIT

This is the long title for the East German intelligence organization known for many years as the Stasi. By popular acclaim among intelligence professionals, the Stasi was considered second only to the KGB among Eastern Bloc intelligence agencies. The Stasi watched not only foreign agents but also its own citizens. It also sent agents into foreign countries. When East Germany fell apart and large parts of the Stasi archives became public, East German citizens were stunned at the details of their lives that had been collected and filed.

7. SPECIAL OPERATIONS EXECUTIVE (SOE)

Though it was officially disbanded after World War II. Britain's SOE makes the list because of its legacy. When people criticize such CIA tactics as overthrowing governments and planning assassinations, few recognize that these are the tactics taught to the OSS people who became the CIA people, when they attended such places as Camp X on Lake Ontario in Canada. SOE would teach anyone who promised to kill Nazis, and that included training Jewish groups in sabotage and the other fine arts of terrorism. After World War II, the Jews turned these tactics on the British in Palestine, and they were just as effective. By the time the Brits left Palestine they were damn glad to get away from the bombers and assassins they themselves had often trained.

8. THE WOLVERINE OF THE INTELLIGENCE GAME—THE MOSSAD

The Wolverine is a compact ruthless bundle of muscle that no creature of the Northern forest, no matter how large, messes with unless absolutely necessary. In the intelligence game, that organization's full title is Central Institution for Intelligence and Special Assignments. Mossad means *institution* in Hebrew. Agent for agent, Mossad is doubtless the most daring, fierce, and ruthless intelligence agency protecting the interests of any modern country. Its reputation and its record are so impressive it's hard to believe that it's so small, with a permanent staff of under 1,500 very talented, dedicated people. This small staffing is possible because of the tens of thousands of *sayanim* (volunteer helpers who receive only expenses), scattered around the globe, who help with everything from surveillance to logistics. There may be 15 thousand *sayanim* in the United States, and as many as five thousand in Great Britain. In the 1950s Israeli taps and bugs were found in the office of the U.S. ambassador to Israel—proving the intelligence adage that you spy on your friends as much as your enemies.

9. MILITARY INTELLIGENCE 6, 007'S OUTFIT

MI-6 is the Secret Intelligence Service (SIS) whose factual and fictional exploits have long formed the background for spy thrillers. MI-6 was founded in 1911 and first headed by the eccentric Captain Mansfield Smith Cummings, the model for the "M" of the James Bond books. He used his initial, "C," to sign documents and as shorthand for his name. To this day the head of MI-6 is called "C." Cummings also used green ink to sign and annotate documents, and even today only the head of the Secret Intelligence Service uses green ink. During World War I, SIS had considerable success with a scheme called "White Lady," which tracked German train traffic in occupied Europe. World War II saw the breaking of the German Enigma cipher, and the destruction of American isolationism. But there were problems as well as victories. Most damaging were the penetrations by Soviet Intelligence, such as the spy Kim Philby. Today MI-6 works closely with U.S. Intelligence.

10. DGSE, THE AGENCY FORMERLY KNOWN AS SDECE—NOTORIOUS, IN A QUIET PROFESSION

DGSE is the French abbreviation for *Direction General de la Securité Exterieure*, the name it acquired in 1981.

DGSE is the French equivalent of America's CIA or Britain's MI-6. They carry out too many highly visible operations for my taste, but to each his own. They are daring. Mingled among several known attempts on the lives of foreign leaders (they made going after Egypt's Gamal Abdel Nasser into a small industry) and several kidnap attempts have been high profile operations such as the sinking of the Greenpeace ship *Rainbow Warrior*.

From Russia with Secret Police

During the 20th century the Russian people, and many non-Russians, have been ministered to by a shifting kaleidoscope of secret police organizations: The Okhrana, the CHEKA, the GPU, the OGPU, the NKVD, the MVD, the KGB, SMERSH, the GRU, the SVR (today's edition—the Russian Foreign Intelligence Service).

Now some, and this includes some Russians, would argue that the Russians are an unruly people with few internalized inhibitions and thus in need of a firm hand to keep them in line. The tough tactics employed have given the Russian secret police a bad name—or a series of bad names. As each name became too stained, a new title was trotted out. The historical record, as you will see, also suggests that anyone who becomes chief of one of these organizations need not burden himself with much retirement planning.

1. OKHRANA (1881-1917)

The Russian tsars had had secret police since the days of the unbalanced Ivan the Terrible in the 1500s. They were used mainly to keep track of the tsars' enemies.

Tsar Alexander II, a kindly reformer, relaxed the grip of the secret police and was rewarded with a bomb in his lap while he was driving near the Winter Palace in St. Petersburg in 1881. His successor, Alexander III, took the assassination to heart, believed most of his father's liberal reforms to be so much nonsense, and took a firm hand. One result of his views was a new and improved secret police, the Okhrana. The word means *guard* in Russian, and the Okhrana did just that for the royal family and government officials. In one sense, this was prudent. This was a worldwide period of explosive growth of revolutionary movements with their concomitant plotting and numerous assassination attempts. Some were successful—in the United States, President Garfield was shot to death in 1881, and President William McKinley was assassinated in 1901.

At any rate, the Okhrana became the first modern powerful secret police organization—a trendsetting pioneer in the arts of infiltrating antigovernment groups, planting *agents provocateurs,* and imaginatively and systematically abusing prisoners. One *agent provocateur,* a Russian Orthodox priest named Father Gapon, led the revolutionary 1905 "Bloody Sunday" mob march on the tsar's Winter Palace. Thousands were killed in an action that many feared would overthrow the government. The revolutionaries eventually executed Gapon after he was exposed by another Okhrana agent trying to save his own neck.

2. CHEKA (1917-1922)—EXTRAORDINARY COMMISSION FOR COMBATING COUNTERREVOLUTION AND SABOTAGE

Felix Dzerzhinsky, once a student for the Catholic priesthood, became the first head of the CHEKA. His wealth of experience as a guest of the Okhrana was put to good use. He combated counterrevolution and sabotage with mass arrests, mass shootings, secret executions, torture, and imprisonment. One of his great achievements was a phony counterrevolutionary movement called the "Trust."

This was a work of genius. It duped foreign governments of their gold, manipulated their foreign policies, and lured anti-Bolshevik agents, including the great British agent Sidney Reilly, to their deaths. The CHEKA was so good that foreign governments did not want to believe they had been fooled, even when Bolshevik agents defected and told them. Ah, the will to believe.

3. GPU (1922–23)—STATE POLITICAL ADMINISTRATION

This was a short-lived nameplate switch, with Dzerzhinsky still in charge.

4. OGPU (1923–1934)—UNITED STATE POLITICAL ADMINISTRATION

Dzerzhinsky was still at the helm at the time of this name change. He was head until his death in 1926 at age 58 (said to be of natural causes). The OGPU oversaw forced collectivization of the Ukraine and the liquidation of the rich peasants, the Kulaks, as many as 9 or 10 million of them. The man in charge during the killing spree was Vyacheslav Menzhinsky. By 1934 the name and the initials smelled awful, so another name change was in order. Menzhinsky was poisoned by one of his ambitious underlings who wanted his job—so much for that logjam at the top.

5. NKVD (1934–1946)—PEOPLE'S COMMISSARIAT FOR INTERNAL AFFAIRS

NKVD served as the new, innocent-sounding name. It came with a new director, the poisoner Genrikh Yagoda (1891–1938). Mr. Yagoda was a man of little education but he was the sort of hard-charging, hands-on manager that Stalin loved, at least for a while. It was Yagoda's plan, his vision, that created the massive, all-intrusive police state, the Soviet/Russian intelligence system we see today.

Yagoda institutionalized and extended the interest in pharmacology he had exhibited in dealing with his former boss Menzhinsky. He set up the NKVD's notorious poison laboratory, even using his spare moments to carry out poison experiments personally. Other moments away from his desk were spent torturing prisoners in the headquarter's cellars. He is also noted for his meticulous preparation of the defendants in the mid-1930s purge trials (show trials), where Stalin had his old Bolshevik comrades and later the officer corps of the military shot as spies.

Yagoda was so good he made Stalin uneasy. This was bad. Stalin had him arrested and shot by Nikolai "The Bloody Dwarf" Yezhov (1895–1938?) As the new boss, Yezhov enthusiastically completed the purges, which had liquidated more than two million Russians by the end of the 1930s. In 1938 that included Yezhov himself, who, word has it, was personally strangled by his successor Lavrenti Beria (1899–1953). It was Beria who was to guide the NKVD through World War II.

Yagoda, Yeshov, and Beria share credit for the phenomenal penetration of the government of the United Kingdom and the United States, everything from the State Department and Foreign Office to the whole British/American intelligence apparatus and the atom bomb project. As is now apparent from the Venona project and the opened Communist archives—they had us covered. Under Beria, the NKVD spent the war shoring up discipline with executions and imprisonment in Siberia.

6. MVD (1946-1954)—MINISTRY OF INTERNAL AFFAIRS

This was only a nameplate change, with the same old killers in charge. Beria's end came in 1953. Most stories suggest that he was shot, either at his desk or by a firing squad. Soviet Premier Nikita Khrushchev later claimed that he personally shot Beria when Beria came into his office without bodyguards. Others say his fellow Politburo members strangled him. There are those in CIA circles who suggest that the CIA floated the rumor that Beria was a CIA asset. Given the endemic paranoia among Soviet officials, this was certainly unhelpful to Mr. Beria's cause.

7. KGB (1954-1991)—COMMITTEE FOR STATE SECURITY

With the end of Beria came a new chief and the traditional new name. After the initial bloodletting after Stalin's death in 1953, the elite agreed to cut down on the willy-nilly killing of one another. However, the new chiefs were still cut from stern stuff. A few highlights:

> *Sergei Kruglov* was said to have personally shot many of those condemned by the purge trials of the 1930s. He lasted less than two years.
> *Ivan Aleksandrovich Serov* had murdered tens of thousands in the areas taken over by the Red

Army during World War II. In an echo of the past, Serov disappeared in the early 1960s and was never heard from again.

Yuri Andropov was most famous for eventually becoming Soviet premier, but remembered in intelligence circles for his groundbreaking work using psychiatric hospitals to relieve dissidents of their sanity.

8. GRU—CHIEF INTELLIGENCE DIRECTORATE OF THE GENERAL STAFF OF THE RED ARMY

In many ways the GRU is a rival of the KGB, but they also work together. These are the "neighbors" mentioned in the NKVD/Venona telegrams sent from Soviet embassies in the United States back to Moscow. The GRU may surpass the KGB in both money and manpower.

With all the fanfare about the reduction of the power of the KGB it has hardly been noticed that the GRU and its mission remains fundamentally unchanged. That mission has traditionally been industrial and economic espionage. Admittedly, the fruits have often had military applications. For example, the Russian cruise missile is such a close copy of the U.S. Tomahawk missile that CIA people call it the "Tomahawkski." Also, one of the real surprises sprung by the Russians on the invading Germans in World War II was the diesel-powered T-34 tank. No other tank could touch its 32-mph speed and maneuverability. The Germans were so impressed that they even tried to copy the engine, without much success. The most likely source of the engine technology was the U.S. Packard Automobile Company. In the early 1930s, Packard had designed such an engine as a prospective airplane engine, but could not market it during the Great Depression. A Packard engineer sold the plans to the Soviets who had the good sense to see that the engine's destiny was on land, not in the air. This was very advanced stuff in 1941. Most modern tanks have a similar engine.

9. SMERSH

Ian Fleming's fictional James Bond would have spent a lot of time in the unemployment lines had it not been for SMERSH. But Fleming had worked for British Royal Navy Intelligence, and he knew the territory. SMERSH is generally said to be an acronym for the organization's motto, "Death to Spies." Its official name was Ninth Division for Terror and Division. Using a wide variety of hard-to-detect methods—electric guns, poisons injected from umbrellas, sprays of prussic acid—this group's record of murder, kidnapping, and blackmailing outside the Soviet Union is unrivaled. Just the assassinations deserve a Top 10 list of their own. True to form, there was a name change. More recently, this little group of charmers has become the GUKR, the internal security department of the Red Army.

10. SVR, THE FOREIGN INTELLIGENCE SERVICE

When the KGB coup attempt of August 1991 went wrong, leading to the demise of the Soviet Union and angry mobs in Dzerzhinsky Square pulling down the giant statue of the sainted Dzerzhinsky himself, the KGB seemed to dissolve. Fortunately for the KGB, the mobs did not break into the building itself and pillage the place à la Rumania or East Germany. (Historians certainly would have had a frolic through the documents.) This led to a fragmentation of the service, at least temporarily and on paper, a new name, and a kinder, gentler public personae. Recently, however, the statue of Dzerzhinsky has been re-erected on a side street, and many of the scattered departments seem to be coming back together. Defectors and blown agents say Russian Intelligence is back in the game, with the only real change being a new emphasis on industrial espionage, long the specialty of the SVR's rival, the GRU.

American Revolution, American Spies

There is a tendency to picture the American Revolutionaries as sort of saintly innocents who with God and righteousness on their side smote the wicked British and won our nation's liberty. In fact, these were tough, worldly, and hard-nosed men. Today it would be very difficult to gain their range of experience without having done some serious jail time. If they seem, in their documents, papers, and the Constitution they later wrote, to be very suspicious of human nature, its lust for power, its failures and flaws, it might well be because they knew themselves.

1. THE LIBERTY CLUBS

After the Seven Years' War (1756–1763), the British took a hard look at the account books on the American colonies and found they had never paid their way. The answer was to impose new taxes that the crown would seriously try to collect. The ill-fated Stamp Act, which mandated that all printed documents, including sermons, wills, and newspapers, purchase and affix a stamp is a fine example of how things went wrong. In fact the Stamp Act so greatly offended the American chattering classes that it brought on America's first intelligence service—The Sons of Liberty—with their secret, subversive Liberty Clubs. Through these, they coordinated resistance—riots, attacks on stamp agents, and destruction of the hated stamps. The British Parliament hastily repealed the hated Stamp Act the following year.

2. THE GREEN DRAGON

The Sons of Liberty organization did not fold up its tent after 1766, but continued as a secret subversive inter-colonial organization. Its membership overlapped (after 1772) with the Committees of Secret Correspondence. By 1774 some two dozen or more of the Boston Sons of Liberty met regularly at the Green Dragon Tavern to trade intelligence on their surveillance of General Gage's four or five thousand occupying troops. Their correspondents in the countryside meanwhile accumulated arms and ammunition and drilled the local militias.

3. GEORGE WASHINGTON—A MAN FOR ALL OPERATIONS

A recent CIA document evaluating George Washington's intelligence operations during the American Revolution (1775–1783) says: "He was adept at deception operations and tradecraft and was a skilled propagandist. He also practiced sound operational security." This report also said of George that he "was a skilled manager of intelligence. He utilized agents behind enemy lines . . . interrogated travelers for intelligence information and launched scores of agents on both intelligence and counterintelligence missions." Washington kept full control over Continental Army intelligence operations, and he was very realistic. He demanded a secret service fund from the Second Continental Congress though he was less than enthusiastic about the paper money they were issuing. He thought gold or silver (preferably gold) best for intelligence work. "I have always found a difficulty in procuring intelligence by means of paper money . . ." he wrote.

Penny-pinching had no place in Washington's intelligence gathering scheme: "Leave no stone unturned, nor do not stick to expense." In contrast to his reputation for never telling a lie, it is startling to review Washington's real performance in this area. In truth the cherry tree chopper was a master of disinformation. He and his wretched troops survived the harsh winter of 1777–1778 at Valley Forge, Pennsylvania, largely because the British General Sir William Howe stayed cozily by the fire in Philadelphia. Yes, he was naturally indolent, but this was reinforced by fraudulent information Washington had planted on Tory spies suggesting that attacking the encampment at Valley Forge would not only be a cold, miserable endeavor but also might be a miserable failure. A similar trick prevented British General Clinton from attacking Newport, Rhode Island, in 1780. Here Washington had a fake plan to attack New York City fall into the hands of a Tory spy, who loyally hustled it to General Clinton. Thinking he was about to be attacked, Clinton stayed in New York City and called off the attack on Newport, where French troops were being landed to reinforce Washington. The landing went undisturbed, and the French troops and naval support were the deciding factor in Washington's victory the following year over Cornwallis at Yorktown, Virginia.

Washington's move south had also been masked

by a leaked fake plan saying he was about to attack New York City. In New York, Clinton just could not get the hang of this. He was again immobilized in New York while the desperate Cornwallis, with no reinforcements or relief in site, surrendered. The British military band emerged from Yorktown playing "The World Turned Upside Down," and I hope I have done the same to your belief in simple, unimaginative George Washington. The American victory at Yorktown ended the war.

4. G-2 AND 1776

Things did not go well in late summer 1776 for George Washington in New York. He was initially faked out by a diversionary attack and only barely able to withdraw with the loss of 1,400 men after British General Howe fell on him with his main force. Washington, realizing his plight, formed a small group of his best men into a reconnaissance unit, "Knowlton's Rangers," to make sure he was not surprised again. Thus, U.S. Army Intelligence marks its founding from 1776. The date is on their crest.

5. YALE CLASS OF 1773

In his book *Cloak and Gown*, Robin Winks, the Yale historian, presents a wonderful catalog of twentieth-century Yale men—Norman Holmes Pearson, James Angleton, and Sherman Kent, to name a few—who have cut an impressive record as founders of modern American intelligence in the OSS and CIA. The Yale tradition goes back as far as September 1776, when George Washington found himself in New York City and desperate for information on the British General Howe and his troops, then on Long Island. Washington asked volunteers to dress as civilians and infiltrate the British camp. Most of his recently formed elite Knowlton's Rangers unit thought this sort of treachery dishonorable and declined. There was, however, one volunteer, Nathan Hale. Perhaps, being a Yale man (class of 1773), Hale was not as troubled as the others by such words as duplicity and treachery. He was also apparently untroubled by the fact that he was utterly, completely unqualified and untrained for such a mission. First, he stood out like the proverbial sore thumb. He was taller than most men and he had a memorable face, distinctively scarred. If that were not enough, his Tory cousin Samuel Hale was a deputy to British General Howe. We know little more of his adventures or his capture, only that he was hanged. In regretting that he had only one life to give for his country, he had one of the great speaking parts in American history.

6. JOHN HONEYMAN, A NATURAL

You will see history books that put words such as "suspicious" or even "sleazy" in the same sentence with John Honeyman's name. In other words, we are in the presence of a natural—a man completely untroubled by the moral quandaries that had beset Knowlton's Rangers when Washington asked them to dress in civvies and infiltrate the British lines. He delivered no stirring speeches after screwing up and getting caught. He delivered good, clear, accurate, timely information on the Hessian troops left behind by Howe at Trenton after his victories over the Revolutionaries. After being chased out of New York City, Washington needed good information so when John Honeyman, an Irish weaver now disguised as a cattle dealer, appeared, Washington consulted with him privately. Out of this little *tête-à-tête* came the general's brilliant attack on the Hessians at

Trenton at Christmas 1776. This was a surprise and a great success, buoying the spirits of Revolutionaries and perhaps saving the Revolution.

7. SPY IS SUCH AN UGLY WORD

One of General Washington's spies was a sensitive man named Hercules Mulligan who preferred to be called a "confidential correspondent" of the general. Good enough. Mulligan was a skilled tailor living in New York and like many artisans had been an early, outspoken advocate of revolution. He was even a member of the Sons of Liberty. Alexander Hamilton, during the Revolution an aide to General Washington, had as a young student lived with Mulligan. Despite these drawbacks, Mulligan was able to use his good contacts within New York—among other things, he made clothes for the British officers—to gather good intelligence and pass it on to Washington.

8. SAVED BY THE TONGUE

On the very day Nathan Hale came to a bad end on a rope, the British caught another spy, an immigrant Polish Jewish businessman named Haym Solomon. The British were about to make Solomon a matched pair with Hale, when they discovered that he could speak six languages including German, just like the troops they had rented from people like the Prince of Hesse. This skill was so useful that the Brits put him to work as a translator and general go-between, until they discovered that he was using his language skills to persuade the Germans to defect to the Revolutionary side. Again, he was sentenced to death but escaped to the Revolutionary side to help finance the war.

9. THE PHONY CULPER JR.

The Culper spy ring, which served George Washington so well, had, of course, no Culpers in it. Samuel Culper Jr. was a New York City tailor named Robert Townsend who even joined the Tory militia. Culper Jr. maintained an extensive stable of subagents. Alas, the tradecraft on this operation was so good that most of their names have been lost to history. All we have are a series of numbers and some cryptic notes.

10. RIVINGTON—THE MOST NOTORIOUS TORY

James Rivington was a notorious Tory. True, Culper Jr. worked as a gossip columnist for Rivington's Tory paper, *The Royal Gazette*, and they were partners in a coffeehouse popular with the king's officers, but had not a Patriot mob burned his papers and offices? His business had been ruined, and he died poor. It was not until the 1950s that scholars finally confirmed that Rivington, the loyal Tory, had actually been a member of the Culper ring.

American Revolution, English Spys

John Adams, later president of the United States, once estimated that one-third of the colonists were for the American Revolution (1775–1783), one-third against it, and one-third neutral. Given these divided loyalties and the shifting fortunes of war it should not be surprising that spies and informants turned up everywhere, and it was well nigh impossible to know whom to trust.

1. A WIFE AND HER MONEY WERE SOON PARTED—THE TALE OF BENJAMIN CHURCH

You remember Paul Revere, the colonial silversmith and engraver. His propaganda engravings of such events as the Boston Massacre did much to generate support for the American Revolution. He had in fact been one of the original agitators for revolution. Like most of his revolutionary compatriots, he would be a very vague figure if not for Longfellow's poem "The Midnight Ride of Paul Revere." He fared well in the poem but less well on the real ride of April 18–19, 1775. In fact, for public relations purposes, he is fortu-

44

nate that his name rhymes better with "hear," than did that of William Dawes, who made the same ride but evaded capture by the British. Revere's first task was to warn Sam Adams and John Hancock at Lexington of the approach of British regular army troops. He did that but shortly thereafter was captured by British soldiers. His companion William Dawes escaped. But Revere was nothing if not resourceful, and his constant chatter about revolutionary militias made his captors nervous; after relieving him of his horse they released him. So there he was with no money, on foot, and far from home. His good wife Rachael became concerned and dispatched a letter and 125 pounds with a trusted friend, Benjamin Church. Who could be more trustworthy? Church was a member of the provisional Congress of Massachusetts and surgeon general of Washington's troops. Alas, he was also a British spy who gave Rachael Revere's letter to British General Gage. The 125 pounds? That seems to have gotten lost.

2. MORE ON THE MOLE, DR. CHURCH

Dr. Benjamin Church was one of the prominent members of the American spy cell, the Green Dragon group of the Sons of Liberty. Unfortunately, he can probably lay claim to being one of the first moles in American intelligence. He returned from London Medical College in England with an English wife and expensive tastes, including a mistress, unsupportable by his practice. Thus, he earned an extra farthing selling information to General Gage. It was intelligence from Dr. Church and others that let Gage know the location of the patriot's weapons stores in Concord. Thus Gage set off with his troops on that fateful 19th of April, 1775. Church seems to have had a talent for fomenting crucial battles;

he also warned Gage that the rebels were going to fortify Bunker Hill. The bad doctor was by chance found out by George Washington. Lacking full evidence of his crimes, the patriots eventually shipped him out to the West Indies. He was never heard from again. Only in the 20th century did scholars searching General Gage's papers piece together the full story.

3. COUNT RUMFORD, BY ANY OTHER NAME BENJAMIN THOMPSON

Under the name Benjamin Thompson this young seeker of the main chance had married a rich widow more than a dozen years older than himself and set about reporting on the American military to General Gage by way of invisible ink. He eventually left both his wife and America for Europe and never looked back. He lived a famous life as Count Rumford the soldier/scientist.

4. ANOTHER KNAVE—PAUL WENTWORTH

As an American, it is hard for me to write about this group without a sigh and the conviction that these 10 spies make up one of the finest collections of knaves ever brought together on paper. Paul Wentworth was the colonial agent in London for New Hampshire, as Benjamin Franklin had been for Pennsylvania and Massachusetts. The colonial agent was a sort of lobbyist/bribe artist who looked after his colony's interests in London. In addition, Wentworth was the London representative for the Revolutionary Committee of Secret Correspondence. Unfortunately, he had been recruited (doubled) by British intelligence and was acting as assistant to the head of the British intelligence service. Fortunately much of this was known to the wily Ben

Franklin, who used Wentworth as much as Wentworth used him.

5. MY FAVORITE KNAVE—DR. EDWARD BANCROFT

Everyone liked young Dr. Bancroft, as do I. He was amiable and he firmly obeyed the 11th commandment of espionage "Thou shall not get caught." Bancroft's motives are as clear today as they were obscure to his victims—500 pounds down and 400 pounds a year, and a 200-pound pension for life (later raised to 500 pounds). These were tidy sums at the time. For this he first spied on the American agent from the Continental Congress's Committee of Secret Correspondence in France, Silas Deane.

The news was juicy; the French had set up what the CIA today would call a proprietary—a phony commercial company serving as a front. This proprietary *Hortalez et Compagne* bought three dozen ships and proceeded to send guns and powder to the rebellious colonies. And that was just the beginning. Bancroft acted as a secretary to Benjamin Franklin at the Paris peace negotiations in the 1780s, so the Brits knew the inside information on the colonist's negotiating position. All this remained secret for a century. Today, however, we have wonderful documentation of Dr. Bancroft's deeds. The doctor himself created the record, in large part because the British were tardy in paying him. So, doing what doctors do best, he billed them for services rendered and a century later the bill surfaced in the British archives.

6. THE SPY WHO DID NOT THINK HE WAS A SPY—MAJOR ANDRÉ

British Major André was returning from confirming that Benedict Arnold would sell out West Point for $20,000, the equivalent of about $400,000 today, certainly a bargain as forts go. Unable to catch his boat, he put on civilian clothes and started on his way but was captured by Washington's troops with the secret papers in his boot. All the signs of a spy, even if he said he was not spying, just bribing an officer of the Colonial army to turn over a fort to him. Washington thought André had taken leave of his senses, being caught in civilian clothes, but nevertheless ordered him hanged, and it was done.

7. BENEDICT ARNOLD—ENOUGH SAID

8. FROM CANADA WITH MONEY

It is now plain that when the British band marched out of Yorktown playing "The World Turned Upside Down," the Revolutionary War was, for practical purposes, over. That is not quite how it looked at the time, though. Washington toyed with the idea of another invasion of Canada, and the governor general of Canada, Sir Frederick Haldimand, feared that Washington would try it. Haldimand told his secret service chief for Vermont, Justus Sherwood, to spare no expense. Sherwood did as he was told. It was a classic case of supply meeting demand. Since Washington had scrapped the idea of an invasion, Sherwood's reports were largely the product of vivid imagination. But good fiction can pay well, so Sherwood kept sending reports. Haldimand was buried in very scary reports of imminent invasion. A fool and his money . . .

9. MAJOR JOHN THORNTON—THE SPY UNCLOAKED

Major John Thornton was secretary to the paranoid Arthur Lee, a member of Benjamin Franklin's treaty-making team in Paris. It is only fitting that Lee, who saw spies and traitors everywhere, should have been saddled with a private secretary who was the real item, British spy John Thornton. Franklin had his own spies back in London, and one of them tipped him that Thornton was a British agent. The French then demanded that Lee, as the employer of Thornton, be recalled as a security risk. He was recalled, much to the relief of the other British spies (such as Franklin's secretary, Dr. Bancroft), who had been made very uncomfortable by all of Lee's accusations that they were spies.

10. THE MISTRESS WITH NO NAME

One of the major problems of intelligence is seeing the true intelligence in the thicket of disinformation thrown up by the enemy. In this case, British General Clinton wanted to believe that the Americans and their French allies were going to attack New York City. Actually, Washington and the French were headed for Yorktown and the decisive battle that would actually end the war. Clinton's secret service received the correct information from the mistress of French Colonel Donatien Rochambeau, the son of the French commander, but Clinton was so in love with the idea of an attack on New York City that no information was persuasive enough until it was too late.

Major Martin and Friends—Those Who Never Were

One nice thing about espionage—you do not really have to exist to make a major impact, even a life-or-death impact, on those who do exist. In this section we will find not only Major Martin, "The Man Who Never Was," but whole armies that existed only on paper and in the minds of the enemy. *Ruses de guerre* is what the French would call the whole lot of these. There is another lesson here: In the 20th century intelligence in most countries is run by bureaucracies, and bureaucracies love bloodless words with all the life sucked out of them. The bureaucratic word for those who do not exist is *nominal*, where the man on the street might use more direct words like *phony, false, bogus,* or *fake.*

1. OPERATION MINCEMEAT

This code name obviously lies outside the realm of good tradecraft. It certainly was not picked from a random list, but so much the better. In brief, the Allies needed a ruse to divert German attention from the true troop-landing site in Sicily in 1943. So the Brits found a dead body and dressed it like a British major, complete with papers saying the landing would take place in Greece.

2. FROM THE PEOPLE WHO BROUGHT YOU OPERATION MINCEMEAT

The XX Committee, also known as the Twenty Committee or the Double Cross Committee, operated from January 1941 until the end of the war in 1945. The guiding lights here were academics—the American representative was Norman Holmes Pearson of OSS and Yale—their minds undoubtedly honed to the task by years of devious departmental infighting. The chairman of the XX Committee, Oxford don Sir John Masterman, attributed the near-perfect attendance at meetings not to the interesting work, but to the tea and "excellent buns" he always provided.

3. PATTON'S FIRST ARMY GROUP

Even with over 200 German divisions fighting on the Eastern Front, the British and Americans could see that if the 65 German divisions in France were rushed to the Allied landing sites in Normandy, things could get very chancy. In fact, there was a good chance the invasion would fail. The solution was to convince the Germans that the Normandy invasion was a diversion and that the main attack would take place later and further north near Calais. To this end, the Allies invented the fake First Army Group, supposedly led by General George Patton, and the British doubled German agents and had them radio phony reports. The XX Committee even planted stories in the papers about unruly American First Army troops in bar fights, and letters to the editor complaining about them. If you go to the Army War College, in Carlisle, Pennsylvania, you can see framed sets of shoulder patches and awards and insignia for this phony army, all in nice display cases just like the ones for real armies.

4. JACK-IN-THE BOX OR JIB

JIB is an inflatable dummy used by the CIA in automobiles to deceive enemy agents about the number of people in a car. Great trick—it worked especially well against the FBI. Former CIA man Edward L. Howard, a Soviet mole, evaded capture while the FBI was following him and his wife on an automobile trip. Somewhere along the route, Mr. Howard jumped out and his wife activated a jack-in-the-box dummy. By the time the FBI noticed the ruse, Howard was on his way to Moscow via New York, Copenhagen, and Helsinki.

5. NOTIONAL MOLE

Critics suggest that James Jesus Angleton, the CIA counterintelligence mole hunter, was fooled into thinking there was a high-level mole in the Agency. If the mole Angleton was hunting was only a figment of Soviet Intelligence's imagination, then this was a great success. The hunt was triggered by a KGB agent, Major Anatoli Golitsyn who defected in 1961. He charged that there was a Soviet mole in the CIA. The critics charge that Angleton's efforts to find the mole, from the early 1960s until his forced retirement in 1974, created more havoc at the Agency than any mole or dozen moles could have done.

6. OPERATION SCHERHORN

This was a brilliant Soviet operation, during World War II, to convince the Germans that 2,500 German troops commanded by a captured officer Oberstleutnant Heinrich Scherhorn were trapped behind Soviet lines at the Berezina River. Scherhorn first made radio contact with the German high command in mid-August 1944, telling of his awful position. The Germans spent considerable resources in men and aircraft trying to relieve this phony group. Two SS groups are said to have been expended in the rescue effort. Hitler even promoted Scherhorn and his officers and gave them medals for their bravery and resourcefulness. Scherhorn became a colonel and received the Knight's Cross. The Russians and British were born to carry out this sort of operation.

7. AGENT BOLVAN

The caper described above is so central to Soviet thinking; the Russians had to have a colorful name for this sort of farce. Therefore, the term is Bolvan or "dummy agent." This word comes from the bolvan or dummy hand in Russian card games. This can also be translated as such wonderfully insensitive terms as fool, idiot, blockhead, or bonehead.

8. OH DONNY BOY

Once again the XX Committee was at work. Agent Garbo was run by none other than Soviet agent and British MI-5 officer Anthony Blunt, the "Fourth Man" of Soviet agents who had penetrated British Intelligence. They had Garbo report to the Germans that he had a subagent Donny, who reported a continuous stream of phony reports on Patton's phony First Army Group. Of course there was no Donny, but the Germans loved these reports and got ready to wait for the "real" Allied attack near the Pas-de-Calais.

9. PUTTING YOUR TRUST IN THE TRUST

The textbooks usually describe the Trust as a large-scale ploy operated between 1917 and 1924 to convince foreign intelligence agencies and émigré, White Russian opposition, that there was within Russia an opposition group that they could work with and support. This was the concoction of Felix Dzerzhinsky, the founder of the CHEKA. (The guy whose statue the Moscow mobs pulled down when the Soviet Union fell. Good symbolism.) The Trust was a wonderful vehicle to get money from the West and to lure foreign agents to their doom, including that "Ace of Spies," British agent Sidney Reilly.

10. THE FBI AS MOTHER OF KLANS

The FBI created a Ku Klux Klan group during the heyday of its COINTELPRO scams to destabilize various groups that it deemed subversive. In a certain southern city, the Bureau set up a rival Klan organization to drain strength from the United Klans of America. By using some unwitting stooges, the FBI was able to grow this notional organization to over 200 members. Question: At what point does a "notional" organization become real even if the members are only—in Lenin's wonderful phrase—"useful idiots"?

A Spy's Walk through London

L ondon is so rich in espionage history it is a pity to pick out just 10 sites to visit. What you really need is Roy Berkeley's *A Spy's London*. He describes dozens of London addresses rich in spy history. Berkeley's writing is knowledgeable and entertaining. Glenmore Trenear-Harvey's article "CAFÉ DAQUISE: A Real Spies' Café?" in issue 5 of *EYE SPY* magazine tipped me to the perfect place for a spy watcher's lunch in a spot close to the South Kensington underground station.

1. *SMALL TIME OBSESSION*—CAFÉ DAQUISE, 20 THURLOE PLACE

Your tour can start or finish here, close by the South Kensington tube station. With its large windows, awnings, and yellow trim this place has enough atmosphere to be in the movies, and it has been—in *Small Time Obsession* (2000). It is frequented by Eastern European types with spooky connections and histories. The attraction for the KGB and GRU types was the great selection of Eastern European adult beverages and the food. One guidebook, *London,* by Andrew

Gumbel, praises the food as an "Outrageously good value [in] Polish food. . . ."

2. STATION XVB CAMO SCHOOL

One block north you will come to Cromwell Road and the Natural History Museum. In the basement there, the craftsmen of Special Operations Executive (SOE) had their "Camouflage Shop." Under the direction of J. E. Wills, an expert in costumes and movie sets, SOE manufactured disguised tools of death and destruction that the SOE agents took with them when visiting Hitler's Fortress Europe. Even the king visited to view the display of goodies.

3. FAKES AND FORGERIES

Having come this far in my book I know you're ready for a little stop here just to the east of the Natural History Museum at the Victoria and Albert Museum. Immediately head for room 46 and its neighbors. Here are the museum's fakes and forgeries of the great statuary of the world. You can get close to copies good enough to give the experts a run for their Ph.D.s. Here in one vast hall is a collection that museum directors might well kill for if it were real. Here is Michelangelo's *David and Moses*, Ghiberti's *Gates of Paradise*—the list seems endless. The bonus is that while the crowds are traipsing around Europe, mauling each other to get a lousy view of the originals, you can have a much closer look at impeccable fakes.

4. DUBOK I

In KGB spy talk a *dubok* is a secret hiding place where spies and their handlers can pick up or drop off documents or money—what the CIA people call a *dead drop* or *dead letter box*. To get a look, continue east one door on Thurloe Place (Cromwell turns into Thurloe Place in front of the Victoria and Albert Museum). Here you confront Brompton Oratory. This is a Catholic church dedicated to Saint Philip Neri, one of the leaders of the Catholic Counter Reformation of the 1500s. The church is impressive, with a 200-foot-high dome and a wonderfully gaudy Baroque style interior. The drop site is just to the left of the small altar inside the entrance of Brompton Oratory. The atheists and agnostics of the KGB seem to have a particularly warm place in their hearts for churches.

5.   **THE PATRON SAINT OF DEAD DROPS**

Continue the short distance on Thurloe Place to Cottage Place. Go down Cottage Place to nearby Holy Trinity Church. The KGB drop spot is in a little garden near the statue of St. Francis of Assisi. It seems that the patron saint of ecologists and Catholic Action kept a keen eye on the KGB booty.

6.   **MI-5 BETWEEN THE WARS**

Now backtrack on Cromwell Road, past the Natural History Museum, to 124 Cromwell Road where British counterintelligence made its home through most of the Great Depression. MI-5 did not need much space. With only two dozen members in MI-5, is it any wonder that Soviet Intelligence had a recruiting field day in Britain during the 1930s? One always wonders about Oxford, since Soviet Intelligence had such great success at Cambridge. Did their recruiting flop at Oxford or was it just as successful as at Cambridge and we never found out?

7. A ROSARY FOR THE ATHEISTS

Now backtrack east on Cromwell three or four streets to Ashburn Place, and go three streets south to Wetherby Gardens. Take a left and a quick right onto Rosary Gardens. Number 3 Rosary Gardens was for years the Soviet Consulate. More recently, it housed the Russian press agency with all its KGB agents under journalist cover.

8. THE THIRD MAN

By my count, the third man was Kim Philby. Continue south on Rosary Gardens to Old Brompton Road. Take a right on Old Brompton, two short blocks to Drayton Gardens. Take a left on Drayton Gardens, and go three blocks to Holly Mews. Turn left on Holly Mews to Grove Court. There you will find the basement flat occupied on and off by one Harold Adrian Russell Philby, accompanied by a childbearing significant other (to whom he was not married) and dogs named MI-5 and MI-6.

9. FROM RUSSIA WITH PRISON TIME

Walk east on Holly Mews to Grove Thistle and take a left. Go to the end of the block to Roland Gardens and simply bear left with the road. Here at number 18 was the home of Anna Volkov, she of the fascist-leaning Right Club and lover of U.S. Embassy code clerk Tyler Kent. It was Kent who stole copies of the secret telegrams President Franklin Roosevelt was exchanging with Churchill. At the time, Kent thought them examples of FDR's collusion with the British against the Axis. He gave samples to Anna Volkov who passed them along to the Italian Embassy from whence they found their way to Berlin. MI-5 had thoroughly infiltrated the

Right Club and so in 1940 Volkov and Kent went to jail where their concerns could not disturb the American public or find their way to Germany.

10. **TO THE RUSSIAN TEA ROOM**

From Volkov's home on Roland Gardens continue north to Old Brompton Road and take a right. The third street on your left is Queen's Gate; turn left. The second street on your right is Harrington. The Russian Tea Room was at number 50 Harrington Road just east of Queen's Gate. Admiral Volkov had been marooned in London by the Russian Revolution of 1917, so he opened the Russian Tea Room here and soon developed a reputation for his excellent caviar and vodka. The right-wing, pro-fascist Right Club, with his daughter Anna Volkov as a prime mover, met in the rooms above the tea room. See item 9 for more of this tale of love and espionage.

Continue east on Harrington Road, counting three blocks on your left to Thurloe Place. You are back to the start at Café Daquise and deserve perhaps a vodka on the rocks for your efforts. There is much more for the spy buff to see in London, so get your maps and a copy of Berkeley's book and have at it.

A Spy's Washington, D.C.

The spy capital of the world has moved to Washington, D.C., along with the money and the political power. The District and its environs do not have the long, full history of London, Paris, Vienna, or Rome, but it is catching up fast. As with London, the 10 locations described here provide only a taste. If you wish to drive or walk it yourself, get a copy of Pamela Kessler's *Undercover Washington: Touring the Sites Where Famous Spies Lived, Worked, and Loved*. Those who wish to sit back and take a tour with the pros can contact SpyDrive via the Internet. On "SpyDrive" you will be in a bus for nearly three hours, and your tour guides will be from the KGB as well as the CIA and FBI men who chased them around the District. You can get the $55.00 tickets from Ticketmaster.

1. THE ANCHORAGE

Let us start at Connecticut Avenue, NW and Q Street, just north of Dupont Circle at a building at 1555 Connecticut called The Anchorage. During World War II, this was an apartment complex. It was the Washington, D.C., home of American lawyer and onetime NFL football player Ernest Cuneo, the liaison who tied together British Intelligence, the White House, the OSS, the FBI, the State Department, and the Treasury Department. Nothing was put on paper. He kept everything in his head. Among his OSS roommates at The Anchorage was Arthur Goldberg, the labor lawyer who ran the OSS labor section and later became an associate justice of the U.S. Supreme Court. Another was a Chicago attorney named George Bowden, assistant director of the OSS.

2. COSMOS CLUB

Go west on Q Street a block to 2121 Massachusetts Avenue, NW. Scores of the intelligence world's movers and shakers have been members here at the Cosmos Club. During part of World War II the club was located at Madison Place, convenient to the White House and much that was happening in World War II intelligence. It later moved here to the former home of Sumner Wells, FDR confidant and an assistant secretary of state. (Wells was forced out of the State Department after rumors got out about a drunken homosexual incident with a sleeping-car porter on a train.)

3. ALLEN DULLES

Now get back on Q and go several blocks west to 2723 Q Street, NW. This was the Georgetown home of Allen Dulles and his wife Clover. Dulles is probably the most famous head of the CIA. He led it during the momentous and successful 1950s, when his brother John Foster Dulles was Eisenhower's secretary of state. And it was here that he lived during the Agency's most spectacular failure, the 1961 Bay of Pigs fiasco in Cuba. He lived here until the end of 1968 when he was taken to the hospital, never to return.

4. WILD BILL'S

Now go to the next block on Q to 28th Street, NW. Take a right on 28th and go left at the next block, which is R Street. It is only one block to 2920 R Street, NW. Here we are at the impressive digs of William Donovan, the head of the Office of Strategic Services during World War II and the man who can in large measure take the glory for founding American foreign intelligence. This is the sort of place befitting a successful Wall Street lawyer. When Donovan moved here, the address was actually 1647 30th Street, NW. This may be the best home in Georgetown, sitting at football-field length from the street. Little Bill Stephenson from British Intelligence and his friends should have been right at home here, as there is such a strong aura of an English country house. Donovan had so many meetings with spooks here that he told his wife to move out to the family farm so she would not be burdened with seeing people she should not know about. In more recent times, this was the home of the late Katherine Graham of the *Washington Post*.

5. DUMBARTON OAKS

Continue west on R Street to 31st. So many things have happened at this mansion, including the founding meeting of the United Nations. The rich former ambassador Robert W. Bliss and his wife Mildred put in the famous gardens. It was here that Israeli spy Jonathan Pollard, a U.S. Naval Intelligence analyst, went for a stroll with his handler one summer day in the early 1980s. Pollard showed the handler some secret docu-

Franklin D. Roosevelt Library, Hyde Park, New York

William J. Donovan, a Congressional Medal of Honor winner
in World War I and a successful Wall Street attorney, headed
the Office of Strategic Services (OSS) during World War II.
Much of the groundwork for the CIA was established during
Donovan's time at the OSS.

ments. This was only the beginning, but too soon Pollard was deep into the great game and he was caught. Mr. Pollard got a life sentence for his work.

6. RAISING A GLASS TO INTELLIGENCE

Continue on R Street to Wisconsin Avenue, take a right, and go to 1721 Wisconsin Avenue, NW, La Nicoise Restaurant. Here, most every day at noon, the gaunt head of CIA counterintelligence James Jesus Angleton had lunch. The story is that he always sat at table number 41. Wonderful lunches were served, fueled by I.W. Harper straight Kentucky Bourbon whiskey, oysters on the half-shell, and lots of other good seafood.

7. 3415 VOLTA PLACE

Go up one more street on Wisconsin and turn left back down 34th Street to Volta Place. There at 3415 is one of the Georgetown residences of Alger Hiss. He was the State Department man identified as a Soviet agent by *Time* editor Whittaker Chambers and by the U.S. counterintelligence team working so secretly in the 1940s on the Venona project to break the Soviet codes. Interestingly, this was later the home of Prescott Bush, the father of President George H. W. Bush, when he was a senator from Connecticut.

8. 3327 O STREET, NW; CYNTHIA SLEPT HERE (WITH MANY OTHERS)

Continue south on 34th Street to O Street, NW. British Intelligence agent Amy Elizabeth Thorpe Pack Brousse, code named Cynthia, worked and slept (part of her work) here. What her list of bedmates lacked in quantity it made up in quality—including an isolationist U.S. Senator Arthur Vandenberg (R-Mich.). He was spoken to softly about the merits of not raising too much ruckus in objecting to the Lend Lease bill, which the cash-strapped British desperately needed if they were to continue World War II. Those interested in a bed-by-bed account of her adventures might well consult Mary S. Lovell's fine book, *Cast No Shadow*.

9. MOST EMBARRASSING MOMENT FOR THE CIA

Continue east on O Street to Wisconsin and take a right on Wisconsin to 1335 Wisconsin Avenue, NW, the Au Pied de Cochon French restaurant. It was here that Soviet defector KGB Colonel Vitaly Yurchenko sat down for lunch with his CIA sitter. He ordered the poached salmon and told the CIA man he was going for a walk—which he did, back to the Soviet Embassy. Perhaps it was just as well because it does not sound like he had the makings of a capitalist. The CIA had supposedly offered him a million dollars and a lifetime income, but his girlfriend had refused to defect. Also, the fact that the head of the CIA, Bill Casey, was bragging around Washington about bagging Yurchenko the defector did not sit well with the Soviet—so he bolted.

10. HISS II

Continue south on Wisconsin to the cultural heart of tony Georgetown, the corner of Wisconsin and M Street, NW. Turn left on M and go two blocks to 30th Street, where you will turn left and go to 1245 30th Street, NW. This is another of the homes rented by Alger Hiss. At least he had good taste in neighborhoods, though the neighborhood was not quite as good when he lived here. Chambers testified that he even stayed with Hiss in this house in 1936 and 1937. Hiss went to jail for perjury. He claimed he did not recall ever meeting a man named Whittaker Chambers.

Still Classified after All These Years

The innocent often imagine that the Freedom of Information Act and tough investigative reporters have revealed all that is to be known. Even academics who should know better assume that there is some sort of "Thirty-Year Rule," that forces the British and American governments to reveal all. Not so. In fact, British secrecy rules are even more strict than in the United States. Some of the real goodies are still closely held after 200 years.

1. PRINTING PRESS MONEY

One of the deepest dark secrets of governments is the printing of enemy currencies during wartime. Since this strikes at the very heart of modern government finance, no one wants to admit to having done this even 200 years ago during the wars against revolutionary France. The wild inflations that destroyed the value of the French Revolution's Assignats and the currency of Napoléon can be directly traced to Britain's massive counterfeiting efforts. Scholars of this subject tell me they meet resistance at every turn as they try to research this British effort against Napoléon and his predecessors.

2. THE TRIAL OF ANNA VOLKOV

Miss Volkov was the anti-Bolshevik daughter of the tsar's last naval attaché in London. She was also the lover of one Tyler Kent, a code room clerk at the American Embassy in London. Kent knew a secret. President Franklin Roosevelt and Winston Churchill, who would soon become prime minister (May 10, 1940), had been engaged in lengthy correspondence, which Kent thought would drag the United States into the war. Kent was taking copies of this correspondence home with him, and Miss Volkov was reading and passing some of it on to the Germans through the Italian Embassy. She and Kent were caught, tried in secret, and both jailed. The transcript of her trial with all its inconvenient truths is closed until 2015.

3. PREM 3/252 5, CLOSED FOR 75 YEARS

Says the index in the Public Records Office. After World War II there was a lively debate in the United States concerning the amount of foreknowledge high U.S. officials had of the Japanese attack on Pearl Harbor. Many relevant documents were and are missing, and witnesses changed their testimony. It was hard to prove anything absolutely. It is now clear, however, that President Roosevelt knew an attack was coming, even if no one has proven that the administration knew the exact timing or target. In the 1990s, British historian John Costello moved the question to the British side of the Atlantic in a book appropriately named *Days of Infamy*. Since Churchill and the British were desperately anxious for the United States to enter the war, what did

Churchill know and when did he know it? Were the Brits reading JN-25 (Japanese Navy 25) the Japanese Navy cipher? Good question. The relevant documents for November 1941 to March 1942 are closed until, well, 2041.

4. PSB D-33/2

This secret strategy paper led President Harry Truman, in 1951, to sign a secret directive establishing the Psychological Strategy Board. This created an independent board to conduct psychological warfare against the Soviet Union. Critics who have seen this document charge that it is elitist, that it advocates uniformity, and that it covers all fields of human inquiry. They even suggest that it is a totalitarian formula for the United States. This explanation may seem vague, but I have never found more than hints about PSB D-33/2's contents.

5. DARK AURORA

The name comes from an apparent Pentagon budget slip-up in the late 1980s. The aircraft was the successor to the SR-71 Blackbird spy plane that succeeded the U-2 flown by Francis Gary Powers. Word is that Lockheed built the super-secret Aurora at its "skunk works," that it flew at Mach 6 and 7, and that it left a weird, discontinuous high-altitude vapor trail. This could be the reason that the SR-71 was retired so quickly so soon after its existence was acknowledged to the public.

6. GREATEST SINGLE INTELLIGENCE HAUL IN HISTORY

The East German Intelligence (Stasi) registry was not supposed to be computerized, but bureaucracies being what they are, it was. With the demise of East Germany, someone apparently sold this registry and various other little gems to the CIA on 1,000 CDs packed with state secrets. Little is known about this trove or what it cost Uncle Sam, but onetime East German Foreign Intelligence chief Markus Wolf calls this "the greatest single intelligence haul in history."

7. SOME NEED A LITTLE MORE SECRECY THAN OTHERS

After World War II U.S. Intelligence financed a Swiss company Crypto AG to make and distribute cipher machines for the newly emerging countries of the world. This would allow the "little brothers" communications security from each other, but the "big brother" would be spared the time and expense of actually having to break their coded messages in order to read them. Far better to have the keys already in hand. Also, by making such easily used machines readily available it was hoped the smaller countries could be steered away from such messy (and secure) things as one-time-pads. Only the barest outline of this caper has graced the public press.

8. CYNTHIA 65-3575

The FBI file of Amy Elizabeth Thorpe Pack Brousse is as interesting for what it still withholds as for what it reveals. The file number prefix 65 tells us that this is an espionage matter, but not much else. Though she is mentioned in numerous books and has been the subject of two of them, looking at her FBI file indicates that the public understanding of her bedroom adventures is only a glance through the keyhole. We know she bedded a flock of important people from foreign diplomats

A "declassified" FBI memo on the surveillance of suspected British agent Elizabeth Thorpe Pack Brousse, still heavily redacted after all of these years.

to American senators, but what is behind the black marks? It has long been suspected that Cynthia made the connection that brought the Enigma cipher machine to Britain from Poland. We know she was in Poland in 1939, that she was working for British Intelligence, and that she was sleeping with officials from the Polish Foreign Office. Is that the secret? Take a look at the sample page released from her file and all that has been redacted (the well-educated way to say blacked out).

9. NEXT ON THE VANDENBERG WATCH

Cynthia was a very good-looking woman, but her successor on the Senator Arthur Vandenberg watch was gorgeous and dynamic. Her name was Eveline Mardon Paterson. Her husband had been lost at Singapore, and she lived in Washington with her two children. It was during her companionship that the formerly isolationist Vandenberg became the major advocate in the U.S. Senate for giving Britain $3.8 billion to save them from bankruptcy after World War II. "Uncle Arthur," as the children called him, then went on to be a major cog in initiating the Truman Doctrine (furthering British interests in Greece), the Marshall Plan, and NATO. My first Freedom of Information Act (FOIA) request for Eveline Paterson's FBI file got one page, but the last digit was a hyphenated four, so I knew that responses that said there was no more in her file were at least inaccurate. Finally, after several more FOIA requests, the FBI gave me more of her file, but the most tantalizing page is the one that is blocked out. I knew J. Edgar Hoover would have more on her. Note that her FBI file prefix is 105— "Foreign Counterintelligence Matters."

10. BUYING ROBERT HANSSEN

Not much has been said about the deal that caught the FBI counterintelligence man, but it is easy to see that the Russians sold him out to American counterintelligence. This much is clear. The Russians gave or more likely sold their Hanssen file to American intelligence. This is a tough business, and Hanssen was the first spy I know of who realized that his Russian spymasters would sell him out when the value of what they could get for him exceeded the value of the material he was delivering. Pretty cold, I know. However, Hanssen's tradecraft was so good that the Russians did not know his identity, and the FBI could not figure it out even after the Russians gave them the documents Hanssen had sold them. The frustrated FBI asked if there were any more, and the Russians had saved the garbage bag Hanssen had put the documents in. Inside was one of his fingerprints. I wonder what that print cost in U.S. dollars.

Companies of the Company

British Intelligence was always good at finding sympathizers who would allow them to run or direct their ostensibly independent organizations. During World War II, British Security Coordination (BSC) attacked American isolationists on a number of fronts. For example, Fight for Freedom, an elite outfit of people such as Dean Acheson (later Secretary of State), demanded in June 1940 that the United States declare war on Germany. Another BSC front was the Non-Sectarian Anti-Nazi League, which was used to attack Charles Lindbergh. Later, the CIA, with its greater supply of cash, also used fronts such as the Congress for Cultural Freedom. The CIA went even further. They simply purchased or created scores of "proprietaries." These are business entities, wholly owned by the CIA, which either do business as private firms or appear to do real business. By the early 1960s, CIA was in the airline business in a big way, with airlines like Civil Air Transport, the Pacific Company, and Air Asia. The big operations, however, were Air America and Southern Air Transport.

1. AIR AMERICA INC.—FLYING THE UNFRIENDLY SKIES

Although Air America masqueraded as a commercial airline, its pilots flew SR-71 Blackbirds and U-2 surveillance planes out of Thailand during the Vietnam War. The familiar picture of the helicopter being loaded with people from the roof of the CIA Deputy Chief of Station's residence in Saigon shows a chopper from Air America. Assets in those days were $50 million (about $300 million in 2003 dollars); the airline directly employed 5,600 people. The pilots were paid nicely for the sometimes hazardous duty, over $200,000 a year in 2003 dollars.

The company acquired Air America in 1949 to keep it from the Chinese Communists. Air America flew air support for CIA operations in Southeast Asia and provided plausible cover jobs for agents. It appeared to be a commercial flying service under contract to the U.S. government. Corporate headquarters were in Washington, D.C., with a regional headquarters in Taiwan. Air America was the largest of CIA's stable of airlines. Only one other CIA proprietary ever made a profit, and that was the company's in-house insurance company. Before you ask—there is no evidence that Air America or its employees made heaps of money in the Asian drug trade.

2. SOUTHERN AIR TRANSPORT

During the Korean War and the French war in Indo-China in the early 1950s, Air America did a lot of U.S. Military Air Transport (MAT) business. The military then shifted the rules, demanding that its carriers be certified. This was an impossible requirement for the

CIA. The CIA's purchase of an already certified airline in 1960, the Miami, Florida-based Southern Air Transport (SAT), solved the problem. SAT was small, it had only two aircraft, and one of them was leased. The CIA quickly split SAT into an Atlantic division to carry on the airline's traditional business to Latin America and the Caribbean. The new Pacific division, using planes leased from Air America, did the heavy lifting on the MAT's contracts. With the Vietnam War winding down, SAT was sold to one of its original owners in the early 1970s.

3. THE SPOOKY INSURANCE COMPANY

The only proprietary other than Air America to turn a profit is the company's insurance subsidiary, Southern Capital and Management Company (SCM). In the congressional investigations of the mid-1970s, this was discreetly called "The Insurance Complex," and so it is. It is a corporation under the corporate-friendly skies of Delaware, but its secure offices, the last I knew, were in downtown Washington, D.C. SCM was created in the early 1960s to insure the uninsurable agents and equipment—particularly the airline equipment used in visible operations. Regular commercial insurance companies are way too nosy; they want way too much information pertaining to people and things for the agency's comfort. This outfit also manages the company's investment portfolio, which I understand has done quite well at certain periods.

4. THE INNOCENTS AT THE NEW YORK TIMES

In a 1977 New York Times series exposing CIA operations, the paper wrote: "Among the more unusual of the CIA's relationships was the one it shared with a

Princeton, New Jersey, concern called the Research Council," run by Professor Hadley Cantril. Oh, that it were so. The fact is that once you have all this talk of democracy, public opinion becomes very important—too important to be left to the public. Owning the pollsters serves at least three purposes for an intelligence agency. The intelligence agency needs scrupulously honest private polls to help it judge the soft spots in the public's belief system so that propaganda can be properly angled. Second, it needs honest private polls to help judge the effects of its propaganda both honest and dishonest. Last, sometimes the public polls must be massaged and tweaked and spun for the bandwagon effects necessary to convince someone to act—such as the U.S. Congress.

For example, one of the major mandates of British Intelligence during World War II was to get the United States into the war. One of the connected mandates was to make sure that the United States had an army ready to go once it could be involved in the war. Voilà—the U.S. Congress passed a draft law in the summer of 1940, despite the fact that congressional mail was running wildly against passage. Why? The polls told Congress that nearly 80 percent of draft age men wanted a draft law so that they would be drafted. Sound a little strange? Not only did British Intelligence have a man at Gallup, David Ogilvy (later a big advertising guru), but he also had sympathetic help—one Hadley Cantril, chairman of the Princeton University Psychology Department. Yes, the same guy the New York Times wrote about in 1977. Cantril wrote to the British Intelligence contact at the White House, David Niles, that he assumed that FDR needed "an approving body of public opinion to sustain him in each measure of assistance to Britain and the USSR." How did Cantril tweak the Gallup polls? ". . . I have tried to influence poll results by suggesting issues and questions the vote on which I was fairly sure would be on the right side."

Those who did good work in World War II for British Intelligence and the OSS often moved on to CIA work in the Cold War. Cantril was one of these. The 1977 *New York Times* article said that Cantril and his associate Lloyd Free ran the "Research Council," and that the council "derived nearly all its income from the CIA. . . ." Free told the *New York Times* that he and Cantril "just sort of ran," the Research Council for the CIA. They did lots of polling outside the United States and even some behind the Iron Curtain. The *New York Times* might also have looked at the National Opinion Research Center (NORC) of Denver and the work Cantril did for them as an adviser and director. The NORC was also deep into polling for the intelligence community.

5. MARKET ANALYSTS, INC.

Since this British Intelligence proprietary did so many wonderfully fraudulent polls for British Intelligence during World War II, it deserves a word. The man here was Sanford Griffith, G.112 of Special Operations Executive, SOE. He and his helpers did many things for British Intelligence—espionage, scripts for BSC's shortwave broadcasts to Europe on WRUL, rough work on suspected saboteurs on the New York docks—but some of the best was the bogus polls showing how much various groups of Americans desperately wanted to help the British. He would conduct a poll of the rank and file members of organizations whose leaders were isolationist. For example, in September 1941 Griffith did a poll at the American Legion meeting purporting to show the pro-interventionist sympathies of the Legion members. The results got two days of front-page play in the interventionist *Chicago Daily News.* The *New York Times* wrote that this was a stunning reversal, for the Legion "has long argued against another war adventure abroad." Another poll showing that 70 percent of the Legion members were against sending troops to Europe was buried. The will of the people.

6. IS ZENITH AS HIGH AS YOU CAN GO?

Into the late 1960s Zenith Technical Enterprises acted as cover for the large CIA station in Miami, Florida. This was the convenient lead proprietary of many used by the company to reach out and touch Fidel Castro's Cuba. What did the island need? Zenith tried to make sure that these needs went unfulfilled. It tracked down and plugged holes in the American embargo. There are suggestions that Zenith helped Castro keep his automobile replacement parts inventory down. The condition of the cars on the Cuban roads suggests that much care and attention was paid to this area. Did every tropical country in the world need to develop a vibrant sugar cane industry, flooding the market with cheap sugar? Agronomists were on the way.

7. THE COMPANY FELT INSECURE

Anderson Security Consultants was founded to provide security for the building of the CIA's headquarters in Langley. This is an obvious need. Without such security, the structure certainly would have seen every enemy, and probably some friendly, intelligence agency vying to build in their bugs. Critics might suggest that Anderson Security Consultants was not needed because we already had J. Edgar Hoover and the FBI for such security work. OK, no smiling, you intelligence people. The CIA eventually took heat from various protest groups because a project named Merrimac was launched through Anderson Security. Merrimac sought to trace the funds and connections of various late 1960s protest groups, which it thought might attack CIA buildings. (This was a time of mass protests at places like the Pentagon and university buildings with the goal of shutting the buildings down.)

8. KERN HOUSE ENTERPRISES

Things went to pieces for the CIA's Congress for Cultural Freedom (CCF) project after 1964 when populist Congressman Wright Patman (D-Tex.) got in a snit because the Agency did not know what to kiss and when or did not do it promptly enough. He blabbed about the CIA use of foundations to funnel money to the CCF in an open hearing where the press had been tipped off. In order for the CIA to get Forum News Service, a press agency, out of the line of fire, its name was changed to Forum World Features and its ownership was transferred from the CCF to Kern House, which was run by an old friend of British and American Intelligence, John Hay Whitney, onetime U.S. ambassador to England. Forum World Features, with its 50-odd newspaper clients, was a wonderful vehicle for planting articles. But it too had to be shut down as the journalistic hounds closed in for the kill in the late 1970s. The bad public relations also created credibility problems for a Forum World Features offspring called the Institute for the Study of Conflict, which the left was anxious to attack. Thirty years ago, the institute specialized in studies of international terrorism.

q. WIGMO

Western International Ground Maintenance Organization was a CIA proprietary officially based in Liechten-
stein. Once you own proprietary airlines you need to
do your own maintenance because of security concerns, and this was the outfit.

10. GIBRALTAR STEAMSHIP COMPANY

Last and least we have a little teaser of a CIA proprietary so the in-crowd can fill in the blanks.

James and the Giant Peach to *Goldfinger*

W riters of thrillers tend to gravitate to the Secret
Service as surely as the mentally unstable become psychiatrists, or the impotent pornographers,"
wrote onetime MI-6 man Malcolm Muggeridge in *The
Infernal Grove*. It should be added that the qualities that
make a sound writer—imagination, analytic ability,
day-by-day diligence, ability to write clearly—are qualities that are also useful to intelligence agencies. Some
of the following found their way into intelligence work
because they had proven themselves as writers; some
became writers by using their experience in the secret
world for plots and color.

1. JOHN BUCHAN (BARON TWEEDSMUIR)

Buchan was already a prominent intelligence insider in
Britain before World War I. During World War I (1914–
1918) he became director of propaganda, and effectively extended that department's reach to the United
States. Later he became director of intelligence. In *The
Thirty-Nine Steps* (1915) Buchan's hero Richard Han-
nay keeps secret documents on the location of the

British Fleet away from the Germans. In *The Power House* (1916), he emphasized the thin veneer of civilization that covered humanity's underlying barbarism. In *Greenmantle* (1916) he prevents Moslem fanatics from welding themselves to the German cause. In *Mr. Steadfast* he thwarts German spying in Britain. During the 1930s Tweedsmuir was governor general of Canada, but still conspiring behind the scenes. When President Franklin Roosevelt delivered his "Quarantine Speech," in October 1937, asking for collective action to stop aggressor nations, Tweedsmuir reported to England that the speech, "was the culmination of a long conspiracy between us. (This must be kept secret.)"

2. SOMERSET MAUGHAM

In World War I, Maugham was a British spy in Europe, America, and Russia. His books are well known, particularly *Of Human Bondage* (1915), but the one of most interest to us is a collection of stories of the Secret Service called *Ashendon*. It is a collection that might be even more revealing of Maugham's experience if he had not burned a number of the stories after Winston Churchill told him they violated the Official Secrets Act. Maugham's experience included being sent to Russia in 1917 by Sir William Wiseman, the head of British Intelligence in the United States. Maugham's assignment was to prevent the Bolsheviks from taking over Russia and making a separate peace with the Germans, thus taking Russia out of the war and allowing all the force of German arms to be transferred to the Western Front. Obviously, this did not work out as hoped, but it did supply material for the *Ashendon* stories.

3. JAMES GRADY

James Grady is said to have worked only briefly for the CIA, but knows intelligence well. His best-known work is *Six Days of the Condor*, which fits well with the paranoia- and conspiracy-ridden 1970s. The movie industry operates under heavy time constraints, so the celluloid rendering was the classic thriller, *Three Days of the Condor*, staring Robert Redford and Faye Dunaway. Condor is a "reader" at the American Literary Historical Society, a CIA front. He and his fellow "readers" are searching literature for plots to be plugged into the CIA computer, both to see if the Agency has a similar operation under way and to supply ideas for future operations. By chance, he has stumbled onto a plot he shouldn't know about. When he sneaks out the back way to get lunch a CIA contract hit team, thinking it has everyone accounted for, kills everyone in the office. Condor spends the next three (or six) days running for his life.

4. STIRRED NOT SHAKEN—THE LIVES OF IAN FLEMING AND COMMANDER BOND

The first of the Bond novels, *Casino Royale,* was written in seven weeks in 1952 in Jamaica as the 44-year-old Ian Fleming tried to divert himself from thoughts about his impending marriage to Lady Anne Rothermere. He seemed trapped; Lord Rothermere was divorcing Anne, perhaps prompted by the fact that she was then pregnant for a second time by Fleming. His hasty writing (his next novel, *Live and Let Die,* took a week less) did not allow for much research. The characters often came from his experience. Fleming's wartime boss at Naval Intelligence, Admiral John Godfrey, became

"M." Insiders say that the description of "M's" office perfectly copies that of "C", Sir Stewart Menzies, head of MI-6. Apparently the description is accurate right down to the green light telling visitors to enter, and Menzies's secretary Miss Pettigrew, who was the model for the fictional Miss Moneypenny. Fleming's hobbies appeared too—deep commitment to womanizing, fine food and drink, and gambling. Lieutenant Commander Fleming even bequeathed his wartime rank to his hero.

5. JAMES AND THE GIANT AGRONOMIST

Wing Commander Roald Dahl had a double life in Washington in World War II. As a pilot with a gallant record, he was assistant air attaché at the British Embassy in Washington, D.C. He also worked for William Stephenson (Intrepid), the head of British wartime intelligence in the United States. The Roosevelts, especially Mrs. Roosevelt, thought him a fine young fellow for a dinner guest at the White House, and he even became an occasional houseguest at their Hyde Park, New York, home.

His real assignment became cozying up to the brilliant but flaky leftist, Vice President Henry Wallace. The VP had made a fortune with his hybrid corn and was a very knowledgeable man on the farm. Harold Ickes Sr., FDR's curmudgeon Secretary of the Interior, probably hit it about right when he said he would not trust Wallace's judgment six feet from a manure pile. British Intelligence became more and more interested in Wallace as it became more and more obvious that FDR would probably die soon (very secret stuff: by early 1944 FDR's blood pressure was 240/140) and that they might be left with Wallace and his anticolonial, leftist friends. In these circumstances, the friendly young British Intelligence agent Roald Dahl stuck tightly to Wallace, even stealing a position paper that, he said, "made my hair stand on end." Wallace had to go, and he did, replaced by the unknown Harry Truman. The events of the 1944 Democratic Convention still leave standard historians scratching their heads about how the vice president was replaced. Dahl went on to a successful writing career. His best known work is a wonderful children's book, *James and the Giant Peach*.

6. A MEMORABLE TRIAL

"From the first moment I saw the little man with the mousy hair and pale, ragged moustache, his very pale blue eyes filmed by suspicion and furtiveness almost as if by a visible cataract, I recognized in him the authentic spy, the spy by nature," wrote Compton Mackenzie in *Greek Memories* (1932). With the publication of this substantial 587-page volume detailing his adventures as a British Intelligence agent in World War I Greece, Mackenzie got himself in substantial trouble. He was the subject of a closed trial and a fine of 100 pounds for violating the Official Secrets Act. This fine and the defense had, he figured, cost him 5,000 pounds ($250,000 in 2003). This was a substantial strain on Mackenzie in the Great Depression. He was forced to sell some of his dearest possessions, and he took a memorable vengeance on British Intelligence in his next book, *Water on the Brain,* a farcical send-up of the Intelligence Service, which he calls M.Q. 99(E). He took an even better vengeance by outliving his tormentors. He died in 1972.

7. CRUSADER TO INTREPID

Ernest Cuneo (Crusader to British Intelligence) lived a widely varied life: NFL football player, lawyer, business owner, intelligence officer, journalist, and author. He was attorney for the two most widely distributed newspaper columnists of the 1930s, 1940s, and 1950s—Walter Winchell and Drew Pearson. During one decade, he earned over $100,000 ($1 million or more in 2003 dollars) a year helping to write Winchell's radio show and column. He was an assistant to New York Mayor Fiorello LaGuardia and wrote *Life with Fiorello*, the basis of the Broadway musical "Fiorello."

He was associate attorney for the Democratic National Committee and, most important to us, Cuneo was the liaison who, during World War II, tied together British Security Coordination (Intrepid), with the White House, the Treasury, the FBI, the OSS, and the Justice Department. Here he not only met his future wife Margaret Watson, one of Intrepid's people, but also made lifelong friends of Intrepid and Ian Fleming. Though Cuneo has been dead since 1988, conspiracy aficionados still put his name on the Internet, and you can find him in Gore Vidal's recent book, *The Golden Age.*

In the 1950s, he bought the North American Newspaper Alliance (NANA), a press service. Yes, with all his connections he did have intelligence people working for NANA. Lucienne Goldberg, who later a literary agent and promoted Bill Clinton's problems by befriending and tape recording Monica Lewinsky, was the only person to interview Lee Harvey Oswald in the Soviet Union. For what it's worth she had credentials from Cuneo's NANA. All his friendships and experience culminate in Cuneo's one known (he was a prolific ghostwriter) spy work. He originated the script that became the James

Bond movie and book, *Thunderball.* His motive was not literary but financial—a way to use funds impounded by the British government and reserved for the production of movies within the United Kingdom.

8. GRAHAM GREENE, TALENT SPOTTED BY HIS SISTER

Greene had clear blue bulging eyes, a taut, spare face and the classic pedigree for MI-6: Berkhamsted School in Hertfordshire (his father was headmaster, which put Graham in an awkward situation), and Oxford. His sister, Elizabeth, a high-ranking member of the Secret Service staff, recruited him. At MI-6, he was a subordinate to Kim Philby whom he liked as a good boss. In late 1941, he was sent to Sierra Leone in West Africa. It was here that he wrote *The Ministry of Fear.* After the war he quit MI-6.

By 1948, another British secret agent, Sir Alexander Korda, had hired Greene to go to the city of Vienna, then a sort of intelligence free-fire zone for the major powers, to research what became the book and the movie *The Third Man.* The Soviets were very suspicious of Greene; they suspected him of being the new MI-6 station chief. Can you blame them? He was an ex-MI-6 man employed by another MI-6 man whose movie production company in the United States had been little more than an annex to Sir William Stephenson's U.S. Intelligence operations during the war. With their good intelligence, they surely knew that Korda's knighthood was for more than his World War II movies. Espionage and intelligence continued to be a major theme in Greene's writing. In *The Quiet American* Greene is critical of CIA operations in French Indo-China. *The Human Factor* (1978) is a full-blown double-agent spy novel set in the Soviet Union.

9. **WILLIAM YOUNGER**

William Mole Younger, a long-serving MI-5 officer, was the son of a member of MI-5, Joan Wheatley; the brother of an MI-5 official, Diana Younger; and the stepson of yet another author attached to MI-5, Dennis Wheatley. Younger was both prolific and varied in his literary output. Starting with highly praised poetry, he produced a travelogue—*Blue Moon in Portugal*—and a number of detective thrillers, the most acclaimed being *The Hammersmith Maggot.* Younger's first novel, *Trample an Empire,* said to be "a small man's right to laugh at his rulers," seemed a little odd for one employed to keep down the laughter. However, it did receive praise from novelist, MI-5 agent, and reviewer Dennis Wheatley, who in fine covert operator style neglected to mention that he was Younger's stepfather.

10. **JOAN JOHNSTONE (MRS. DENNIS WHEATLEY)**

Under the names Eve Chaucer and Joan Grant, Joan Johnstone wrote a number of novels including *No Ordinary Virgin, Life as Carola, Silksheets and Breadcrumbs*, and also two children's stories: *The Scarlet Fish and other Stories*, and *Redskin Morning.* Here we really have the family that spied together. With the outbreak of World War II, she joined her son and daughter by an earlier marriage, William and Diana Younger, in the British Security Service MI-5.

noms de Plume and d'Espionage

J oan Johnstone (Mrs. Dennis Wheatley) brings us to another interesting case, the experienced intelligence officer and writer who would find it more convenient if the general readership did not know his or her real name. Their employers often have similar feelings, and a pseudonym is born. Here are the everyday names followed by the pen names of some writers on espionage.

1. E. HOWARD HUNT

Hunt was also known as Robert Dietrich, John Baxter, Gordon Davis, and David St. John. During his intelligence career Hunt was in on many operations, ending, of course, with the blown Watergate caper. Hunt's name is the one the Richard Nixon actor gags on in the movie *Nixon*. This goes against the rule of thumb that an intelligence officer should not be known for his operations.

2. EDWARD SPIRO

E. H. Cookridge Spiro was a Central European resistance fighter who worked undercover for MI-5 in the

British camps for enemy detainees. Under the name E. H. Cookridge he became well respected for his political reporting, particularly his reporting on Parliament. His books include *The Third Man.*

3. JAMES MacCARGAR

Christopher Felix MacCargar was a former CIA man. Among his books: *A Short Course in the Secret War* (1963), also published in London as *The Spy and His Masters: A Short Course in the Secret War,* and *Three-Cornered Cover* (1972), which he wrote with George Marton.

4. RUPERT ALLISON

Allison is Nigel West to the readers of his generally non-fiction books on spies and the spy business. He has good connections on both sides of the Atlantic and writes prolifically and authoritatively. He is close enough to American intelligence to have been among the dozen or so, including the CIA director, who attended a private birthday party in Washington for one of the trailblazers of the CIA, Walter Pforzheimer. Allison's unique gift to Pforzheimer: a framed letter signed by British King George II and Prime Minister Robert Walpole authorizing money for intelligence work. It may also help that he is an MP, a member of the British Parliament. Among his more than a dozen nonfiction books are *MI-5: British Security Service Operations 1909–45; MI-6: British Secret Intelligence Service Operations 1909–45;* and *Secret War: The Story of SOE.* Fiction includes *The Blue List, Cuban Bluff,* and, what else for an MP, *Murder in the Commons.*

5. DONALD McCORMICK

During World War II McCormick (whose pen name is Richard Deacon) was in the British Navy and worked for Ian Fleming of Naval Intelligence. A journalist both before and after the war, he has written some 50 books, as both Donald McCormick and Richard Deacon, including *A History of the British Secret Service* and *A History of the Chinese Secret Service*.

6. DAVID CORNWELL

Better known as John le Carré, Cornwell is a prolific writer whose best known works include *The Spy Who Came in from the Cold; Tinker, Tailor, Soldier, Spy*; and *The Russia House*. He is also an accomplished artist and the illustrator of *Talking Birds* by the head of MI-5's counter-subversion department. Cornwell worked for both MI-5, the British FBI, and MI-6, its CIA. In his MI-6 work he appeared to be second secretary in the British Embassy to the German capital at Bonn. During the erection of the Berlin Wall, he helped rescue agents. In his first two novels, *Call for the Dead* (1961) and *Murder of Quality* (1962), he introduced the aging agent George Smiley who has gotten such a good run.

7. JOHN CREASEY

Creasey's pen names include J. J. Marric, Michael Halliday, Gordon Ashe, Anthony Morton, and a plethora of other names on more than 500 books. Among Creasey's many jobs was reportedly a stint in intelligence work. His first book on the subject was *Death of a Miser*.

8. RICHARD HENRY MICHAEL CLAYTON

Under the name William Haggard this author produced more than 25 books in the 1960s, 1970s, and 1980s, many published in Britain with such titles as *Yesterday's Enemy* and *Visit to Limbo*.

9. **ANDRE LEON BROUILLARD**

Writing under the name Pierre Nord, Brouillard made his literary reputation after World War II with books on the Resistance from the perspective of a participant. However, his first book had come a decade earlier with *Double Crime sur la Ligne Maginot*. Several of his post-war books were part of a series called *Les Chronicles de la Guerre Subversive*.

10. **GILBERT HIGHET SPIED, HELEN MacINNES WROTE**

Highet and MacInnes were a husband-and-wife team. Highet, a respected classics professor at Columbia University, ran Latin American operations for William Stephenson (Intrepid) and British Security Coordination (BSC) in New York City. His wife was the spy fiction writer Helen MacInnes. Her World War II books, such as *Above Suspicion*, *Assignment in Brittany*, and others drew suspicions at BSC that Highet was tipping his wife about operations.

The Monster Rally, Dirty Tricks, and Black Propaganda

The term "Monster Rally" comes from the innovative work of longtime CIA man and novelist E. Howard Hunt. In the movie *Nixon*, it is Hunt's name that the president chokes on when told of the participants in the break-in at the Watergate Apartments. Hunt had been in on so many capers. He had so much baggage. He even bore a resemblance to one of the hobos picked up and released by the Dallas police behind the grassy knoll at the Kennedy assassination—as the Nixon character's reaction seems to indicate he knew. The British, who had often attended those prank-ridden boys' public boarding schools, were particularly good at what they called "vik." Many of these stunts do have the air of school pranks run wild.

1. E. HOWARD HUNT DOES THE MONSTER RALLY

When Hunt was stationed in Mexico he found that a Communist front group was going to give a dinner to honor visiting Soviet dignitaries. He got hold of an invitation and had a printer make several thousand copies, which he had distributed all over the city. The promised free drinks and food quickly ran out, and the doors had to be barred to the angry mob. Guests and host came away with distinctly uncomradely feelings for each other. Fellow CIA officers thus dubbed Hunt's efforts "The Monster Rally."

2. FATHER OF MONSTER RALLY

Actually there was a very good precedent for Hunt's work. During World War II, British Security Coordination (BSC)—the outfit run by William Stephenson—spent much of 1940 and 1941 trying to involve the United States in World War II and thus trying to destroy those who wished to stay out of the war. One of their targets was the American hero and America First supporter Charles Lindbergh. Lindbergh was an ardent anti-interventionist, and his speeches drew huge crowds. For his October 30, 1941, Madison Square Garden speech, BSC went beyond the usual planted hecklers and printed a duplicate set of tickets, hoping to create fights and turmoil over the seating. However, the crowd was smaller than anticipated and the ushers more alert, so all BSC apparently did was to promote the flyer's speech.

3. THE BLACK BOOMERANG

During World War II, British covert or "black" propaganda people were looking for any possible way to sap the effectiveness of the German armed forces. So they had Dr. J. T. McCurdy of Corpus Christi College, Cambridge, pen a little pamphlet for the health-conscious describing symptoms of maladies that doctors had great difficulty diagnosing. Titled *Krankheit rettet* by Dr. med. Wohltat, or *Sickness Saves You* by William Benefactor, M.D., this idea-filled booklet was laid out by the number of days the reader wanted out of the war. Did he want a day off? A week? Did he want out of the war completely? The booklets were duly dropped on the German troops. This was so well done and the Germans were so impressed that they had the booklet translated back into English and dropped on Allied troops. The real killer came after the war when the British Labor government went to socialized medicine and this little tome became an underground best-seller.

4. BARIUM

This is a little trick pulled on their own people by a country's counterintelligence officials. It is a KGB term named after the solution doctors introduce into a patient's intestinal tract so that the flow of bodily fluids can be traced. To the KGB, it is phony information given a suspect in their own government so that the flow of information to Western intelligence can be traced. If the dose of barium is detected the lucky official will be quickly shot. The unlucky may take longer.

5. NAZIS FOR THE GULLIBLE

In the early 1960s the Soviets were becoming alarmed over the close military ties that were developing between West Germany and Britain. When a West German tank group was sent to Wales for practice, the KGB had the Czech State Security Service, the STB, use an agent in Wales to paint swastikas on Jewish graves. This caused a great press uproar in Britain, and the German troops got the blame.

6. BLOWBACK

At the end of World War II the Allies feared that the Nazi brass was sending large amounts of money to Argentina and that they would shortly follow. The FBI thoroughly investigated this in the 1940s, and although some Nazis fled to South America, no evidence was found that vast fortunes to rebuild the Third Reich went with them. The culprit behind the rumors turns out to be that wonderfully imaginative British black propagandist, Sefton Delmer. In 1944 and 1945 Delmer's fertile broadcast group created the phony German General Spraggett to broadcast from their equally fraudulent "Radio Atlantic." This station purported to be broadcasting shortwave messages from Germany to Argentina. Actually, it was near London. Its messages were designed to sap German troop morale by suggesting that their leaders were about to abscond to Argentina. Officials in the United States were also deceived because the OSS chief in London, Bill Casey (later head of the CIA under President Ronald Reagan), who knew what Delmer was doing, failed to pass the word along to Washington.

7. DELMER'S RED CIRCLE

One consistent theme running through Delmer's work was that there were cells of people throughout Germany who were loyal Germans but who were anti-Nazi. One of Delmer's "notional," or phony, resistance groups was the "Red-Circle." All their supposed pamphlets were duly stamped with a red circle. One of Delmer's services to the German military was to publicize a supposed German army order giving a soldier the right to visit his home if it were hit by a bomb. He also thoughtfully attached very accurate, newspaper-sized alphabetical lists of streets in each city that had been hit by Allied bombs. The lists were so accurate that the German authorities began to believe there were swarms of Allied agents in Germany. They spent a lot of effort looking for them and of course hassled a lot of innocent people. Delmer's staff had made the street list from aerial bomb damage photographs and debriefings of aircrews.

8. STOPPING THE NIGHT SHIFT

One of the awful miscalculations of British Intelligence was the belief that German industrial production had been straining at full capacity on the eve of World War II in 1939. If this had been true, then the British blockade and bombing should have had great affect. They did not. In fact German factories had much unused capacity and rarely ran night shifts early in the war. Despite heavy Allied bombing of both factories and civilians, German production actually peaked well into 1944. Since the Nazis thought a woman's place was in the home, they only late and reluctantly put women on night shifts. One of Delmer's efforts to cut into this night-shift production was a wanted poster with a front and side view of the Gauleiter Fritz Sauckel, who had organized these night shifts of women. The poster says that at least 56 women died every night and it offers 100,000 German marks for Sauckel. The last line says, "The women killer Sauckel has to be made harmless" [killed].

9. THE PHONY NURSE LETTER

Sefton Delmer's continuing efforts to destroy German civilian morale always returned to two themes: that the leaders were going to skedaddle and/or that they were lazy and crooked. In the phony nurse ploy, the British forgers were careful to find a soldier's date of death. They would then write a letter addressed to the dead soldier's relatives, purporting to be from a nurse. In the letter, she would tell them that the deceased had collected some wonderful gifts for his relatives. She had personally handed the gifts over to a Nazi official at the hospital for conveyance to the relatives. Of course, the nonexistent presents never arrived and the relatives would be led to speculate that Nazi officials were stealing from dead heroes.

10. BUT NOT TOO LARGE

Nothing was too bizarre or outrageous for Delmer and his largely native German staff. One young Jewish girl refugee, who was helping as an artist, remembers her first day at the Political Warfare Executive. She was directed to a room where a dozen silent people were passing around a postcard: "It was a picture of Hitler in Lederhosen, sitting with his hands folded in his lap, and with the words, written underneath, 'Was wir haben, halten wir' (What we have we hold)," she said. "Finally somebody spoke, 'Look at the picture. You will paint a penis into the hand of Hitler, but do not make it too large.'"

Sobriquets

This is the big word you learn in college that means *nickname*. One advantage of nicknames is that they often capture some quality or sense of irony that the official name is lacking and thus, no matter how politically incorrect, enlarge our understanding. This is far truer in the field of intelligence than in other fields, since the official names have often been deliberately chosen to obscure the real function of the organization or person. Here are 10 of my favorites, many of them culled from the thousands of entries in Leo D. Karl's *The International Dictionary of Intelligence.*

1. "BLU U"

This commemorates the color of a building on Glebe Road in Arlington, Virginia. At this CIA training center, the faculty imparts to the students the practical arts of black bag jobs ("locks and picks") and "flaps and seals" work (opening letters without leaving any unseemly tears or smudges, which might annoy some sensitive recipients). They also teach a good photography course here, though the curriculum may be a little narrow for the real enthusiast.

2. CHILDREN'S WORLD

Detskiy Mir is the name the Russian people have given, with their sense of the absurd, to the KGB headquarters *cum* torture center and execution site, the Lubyanka. The name is taken from the fact that a real toy store is located on the opposite side of Dzerzhinsky Square.

3. GREAT WHITE CASE OFFICER

The CIA people gave Allen Dulles this nickname during his heyday as CIA chief in the 1950s.

4. MOBY DICK

The informal name given the CIA/Air Force program to float high altitude balloons over the Soviet Union was Moby Dick. The balloons were launched from West Germany and picked up in Japan. Those in the know say some excellent photographs were obtained, but the program was superseded in the mid-1950s by the U-2 plane, which was quickly noticed by the Soviets. After a concerted effort, they brought Gary Powers down, U-2 and all.

5. NO KNOCK, THE FISHERMAN, ORCHID

These were the CIA nicknames for James Angleton. He had the ability to walk into the director's office without knocking. This is how you know you have arrived, wherever you work. The other names come from his private obsessions with fly-fishing and growing orchids. According to Robin Winks in *Cloak and Gown*, Angleton is recognizable in more than a dozen novels, one of them appropriately titled *Orchids for Mother*, by Aaron Latham

6. PALACE OF AMUSEMENTS

In compiling this list I was struck by the number of Russian nicknames that are full of much more bitterness and irony than Americans can typically muster. Did Communism do this or is it the weather? At any rate, the "Palace of Amusements" is the nickname for the KGB headquarters of the Kremlin Commandant inside the Kremlin walls.

7. TASTEE FREEZE

The oddly shaped auditorium located on the CIA's campus at Langley, Virginia, is called "Tastee Freeze" by agency employees.

8. BLUEBIRDS

These are the colored buses used by the CIA to transport groups of CIA people to the various company installations around Northern Virginia.

9. COFFIN SQUAT

Remember those tool kits and firearms that fit in a body cavity? The "Coffin Squat" is the name given for your position as the authorities check for those little items.

10. LA PISCINE

Literally, "The Swimming Pool." The French call their external intelligence agency, the DGSE, La Piscine, because one is located close by.

Swallows and Honeytraps

These are the Russian terms for women sent to persuade men to cooperate with an intelligence agency. However, the Russians are not alone, and the technique is not new. In the Bible, Delilah used Samson's lust to wangle from him the secret of his strength. For this Samson's enemies paid Delilah 1100 pieces of silver. More recently, in the mid-1970s, FBI official William Sullivan tried to explain the facts of international life to the prim Senate Church Committee then investigating the activities of American intelligence agencies. The use of sex is, Sullivan told them, a "common practice among intelligence services all over the world. This is . . . a tough, dirty business. . . . We have used that technique against the Soviets. They have used it against us." Sullivan was right, of course. Everybody does it, but, as we will see, the Eastern Europeans seem to positively revel in it. However, let's start at home.

1. SASHA

Sasha was a summer seminar student attending Yale. She was exotic, to say the least, and stylish, with a personal but impeccable sense of taste in clothes, food, and drink. She already had a master's degree, spoke several languages, had gone to fashion school in Rome, and lived for extended periods of time in a multitude of countries. Her looks were Mediterranean, her figure was good, and her dark attractive eyes sparkled. Her wry smile informed anyone who looked more than casually that here was no beginner.

One day the guest speaker in her Yale class was Vladimir Pavel (not his real name, but then again his "real" name was not his real name either), a Soviet diplomat working at the UN. He made contact with those eyes as he walked to the front of the class. She spent the night with him. The FBI also noticed and quickly approached her, making a successful appeal to her patriotism. From 1985 to 1987 Sasha made frequent FBI-encouraged trips to New York City, where she would borrow a relative's apartment for some privacy. The high point came when the upscale school where she taught in Ohio invited Pavel to speak. He flew into Cleveland where she wined and dined him in the Flats, and the FBI propositioned him.

There were some terrible Keystone Cops miscues. In retrospect, these might have been expected. Robert Hanssen, the famous long-term KGB mole inside the FBI, flew into Cleveland from New York to personally run this project. For starters, soon after Pavel arrived at the best hotel in town to meet Sasha, the phone rang. It was the desk clerk. Pavel, said the clerk, had been given the wrong room. It was a corner room, and the FBI wanted them to have a room in the middle of a hall where surveillance teams could occupy the empty rooms on either side. Second, the FBI men had preceded them to the restaurant and told the *maitre d'* that they were waiting for a couple. It was early and business was slow, so when the couple arrived the helpful *maitre d'* pointed out their friends (the FBI surveillance team) who were waiting for them. Vladimir did not take this well at first, but did raise his glass across the room in mock salute. When Sasha went to the ladies' room as the FBI had requested, the agents closed in. They were still at the table when she came back.

Later she could see that the messages from both sides were largely disinformation. On the night the Hanssen story broke, she got a call from her FBI man. Had she seen the papers? "Well, yes," she laughed. It was fully believable. As for Vladimir, the last she knew he had been transferred from the glitter of the Big Apple to Upper Volta. She continued teaching. How many of her students must have failed to recognize the patriotic intelligence swallow in their energetic and perfectly dressed teacher.

2. THE ONE THE SPYCATCHER DIDN'T CATCH

In his book *Spycatcher,* former British MI-5 official Peter Wright tells of his attempts to set a "honeytrap" for a senior KGB official he calls Grigovin. Wright called the proper branch of British Intelligence that "had a number of high-class call girls they used for entrapments. . . . Grigovin took the bait perfectly." Unfortunately, his interest was not love but only frequent sex. There was "little chance to play on his heartstrings," said Wright ruefully. So MI-5 broke in on the lovers, hustled the girl out, and high-pressured Grigovin. He would not change sides and only gave his name, rank, and serial number. After a couple of hours the Brits gave up, tossed him his clothes, and left. "Months of planning and years of patient waiting were wasted," wrote Wright.

3. EVA BOSAKOVA

Eva Bosakova was truly a star, a rare talent—a gold medalist in the balance beam event at the 1960 Olympics in Rome and a movie actress, both legitimate and otherwise. In *The Dictionary of Espionage: Spookspeak into English*, Henry S. A. Becket says Eva was an "agent of long standing, used primarily for the production of compromising films of a sexual nature."

4. CLOSE YOUR EYES AND THINK OF THE STANLEY CUP—WELL, ALMOST

During the 1960s the Czech hockey team was threatened with sure defeat in a major world tournament in Prague by a Western Hemisphere team that shall remain unnamed. His patriotism and Czechoslovakia's honor on the line, the head of the secret police rounded up all of Prague's best-looking prostitutes and sent them to the visiting team's hotel. In the finals the next day, the Czechs won handily.

5. SIR GOEFFREY HARRISON, BRITISH AMBASSADOR TO THE SOVIET UNION

In 1968 the ambassador discovered the charms of a comely embassy maid named Galya, who, after a while, informed his excellency that the only way to avoid distribution of photographs of their lovemaking was to provide information to the KGB. Sir Geoffrey went instead to British counterintelligence. This all seemed fairly routine to MI-5 until the ambassador confessed that he had been having intercourse with Galya in the embassy laundry room. The thought that embassy security was so weak as to allow such photography caused consternation, until later, when Sir Geoffrey remembered that he had also had sex with her in her brother's apartment in Leningrad. No action was taken against the ambassador. He retired on a full pension.

6. MARGARETHA ZELLE (1876–1917), THE MOST FAMOUS OF THEM ALL

Zelle did not achieve fame under her real name. Her *nom de dance*, Mata Hari, is familiar to one and all. Born in Holland, at age 19 she married an officer in the Dutch Colonial forces and went with him to the Dutch East Indies (today's Indonesia) where she learned how to dance like the temple dancers of Java. She returned to Europe, divorced, and made a big splash in Paris with her nearly nude renditions of these dances. This brought her a series of wealthy lovers as she performed all over Western Europe. She was considered to be one of the most expensive sexual companions of her time. Unfortunately for her, in 1914 she was entertaining higher-ups in both France and Germany. She was in Germany when the Great War broke out. By 1915 she was back in Paris and under surveillance by French counterintelligence. By 1916, she had moved on to Madrid where she entertained both French and German diplomats. Her downfall was a German wireless message asking for money for Mata Hari in a code that was known to be broken. Apparently the Germans suspected her of being a double agent and were setting her up to get shot. The French obliged. This is a tough business.

7. COMMANDER ANTHONY COURTNEY

Commander Courtney was well traveled, spoke fluent Russian, and was known from his navy days as a tough customer. He had, in fact, been the head of the Russian section of the British Naval Intelligence Division. However, it was his days as a Member of Parliament and his persistent attacks on Soviet espionage's use of diplomatic cover that brought him problems from the KGB. While on a trip to the Soviet Union the commander was bedded by his Intourist guide, a practiced KGB agent, Zinaida Volkova. Shortly, of course, it was suggested to him that if he did not stop his attacks, photos would be distributed showing him having sex with the lovely Zinaida. He would have none of it, and continued speaking out. It does seem hard to blackmail retirees with pictures showing them having sex with twenty-something women.

8. FULL TREATMENT FOR FRENCH AMBASSADOR

The situation has all the classic elements of a set-piece Eastern European entrapment ploy. KGB informants had fingered French ambassador Maurice Dejean as a vulnerable "ladies' man." They then had a string of beautiful women happen into his path at legitimate-looking parties and receptions. They even went with the traditional step that should have told the mark that he was getting the full treatment.

While having sex, the couple is burst in upon by a KGB man posing as the beautiful swallow's husband, unexpectedly returned. The "husband" takes some swings and threatens legal action. The wife begs. The husband lets the lover go. The film crews that worked the cameras on these operations should have been able to rate the participants after a while. Next, Ambassador Dejean consulted a Russian "friend" about his love predicament. The "friend" was in the KGB. Of course, this situation could be hushed up. And it was. The KGB was

Wendell Willkie, the Republican candidate for president who lost to Franklin Roosevelt in 1940, became smitten with Madame Chiang Kai-shek. During their affair and under her influence, Willkie helped raise money for United China Relief. She and her husband subsequently lined their own pockets with much of the aid money.

just putting the ambassador under obligation, to be called at some future date. The plan was short-circuited when a Soviet defector told British Intelligence and the Brits told de Gaulle, who fired Dejean in 1964.

q. THE DRAGON LADY AND THE BAREFOOT BOY FROM WALL STREET

In late 1942, President Franklin Roosevelt sent Wendell Willkie as his personal representative on a round-the-world tour. Willkie was his defeated Republican rival from the 1940 presidential election. Willkie, almost forgotten today, was a Clintonesque character. He was a charismatic, quotable showman loved by the media. He was also very sexually active. May-ling, a member of the powerful Soong family, was also Madame Chiang Kai-shek, the wife of the autocratic ruler of China. She and Chiang did not get along well, what with his mistresses and everything. However, they were mutually devoted to getting large amounts of U.S. aid money. May-ling, the model for the Dragon Lady in the popular cartoon strip of the time "Terry and the Pirates," had an insatiable appetite for attention.

Providentially, Willkie was able to fulfill both of these needs for the Chiangs. Foreign Service officer John Patton Davies was a witness and wrote of Willkie: "There is little doubt that Little Sister has accomplished one of her easiest conquests . . . It's interesting the influence which enforced celibacy has on judgment—and on the course of political events." That wonderful cynic President Franklin Roosevelt later jovially chided May-ling for taking advantage of Willkie. To which she responded that Willkie had "responded as any adolescent would." The gung-ho, very pro-China speech that Willkie delivered on his return to the United States was wildly simplistic. But Willkie was so taken that he became a board member of United China Relief, which quickly collected $17 million (the equivalent of almost $200 million in 2001) all of which quickly disappeared into China and the hands of the Chiangs.

10. EIGHTEEN YEARS FOR A PROMISE

Mordechai Vanunu worked at an Israeli nuclear plant at Dimona in the Negev Desert for nine years. While there he collected a fine trove of documents. When he was laid off in 1985 he took this archive and ended up in London telling the *Sunday Times* fascinating stories about 200 nuclear bombs that Israel had in storage—far more than outside experts had guessed. Before he could tell them more, a good-looking American blonde named Cindy lured him to Rome with the promise that he would get sex, or more sex, than she had already given him. Unfortunately Cindy was from the Mossad and our protagonist ended drugged and in chains on an Israel-bound yacht. Upon his arrival he was tried in secret. Only a court report was issued and that said that he got 18 years in prison.

Ravens or Swans, the Male Swallows

Though Americans rarely seem to think of sending men as sexual agents, this is not true of the European scene, especially after the millions of battle deaths in World War II caused a lopsided male/female ratio. The Russian term for such men is *voron*, which translates as *raven*.

1. OPERATION DEEP ROOT

In the late 1960s, the Royal Canadian Mounted Police managed to photograph the wife of a Soviet diplomat having intercourse with one of their "swans." They tried to get her to become an informant, but she refused and decamped for the USSR.

2. THE "DON JUAN OF THE NILE"

Mrs. Janet Rhona Ritchie was a vivacious high flyer destined for big things in the British Foreign Office. Posted as first secretary at the embassy in Tel Aviv, she met Rafaat El-Ansary, a handsome young man from the Egyptian Embassy. An affair quickly blossomed and soon they were an item at all the best cocktail parties. He was interested in her work, so she showed him a few telegrams that came across her desk. If British

counterintelligence was napping, the Israeli Mossad was
not, and tipped off the British. Mrs. Ritchie ended in the
dock at the Old Bailey for violating the Official Secrets
Act. Though her prison sentence was suspended, she
had to resign. Mr. El-Ansary was promoted to a plum
posting in Vienna.

3. OPERATION RUBBER DUCK

The Czechs called this one Operation Rubber Duck. In
the late 1950s, Czech Security discovered a middle-
aged foreign woman who worked for a foreign embassy
and who "liked young men, fast cars, and alcohol."
Czech security obliged with a handsome young gigolo,
and it was love at first sight. But the Czechs wanted a
real hold on her, so they set her up to commit what she
would believe was drunken vehicular homicide. Actually, the "old man" she hit as he suddenly stepped out
at a turn was a rubber dummy full of a red liquid. Instead of stopping, she gunned her fast car, outran the
security people, and bolted past her embassy guard.
Her embassy quickly sent her home. And Czech Intelligence cried over the spilled paint.

4. MEN FOR ALL SEASONS

In his book *Touchlines of War*, Sir Peter Tennant tells of
how desperate MI-6 was to keep on top of events in
Sweden during World War II. The Swedes were in an
uneasy neutrality between Germany and Britain and
her allies. The Brits did not like the fact that the Swedes
were supplying industrial goods such as ball bearings
to the Germans, but could not stop them for fear of
pushing the neutral country further into German collab-
oration. Tennant says that SIS found first-class, tennis-
playing, homosexual agents to get information from
the homosexual, tennis-playing German agents who

were playing on court and off with the homosexual Swedish king.

5. BONN OUT OF BALANCE

The post–World War II German population had a very lopsided sex ratio. Six million Germans, mostly men, had been killed in the war. Bonn, West Germany's artificial capital, was even worse with the great influx of women clerks and secretaries in the late 1940s and '50s. The Communist spymasters were not long in supplying this demand for male companionship. One day in 1959, Leonore Heinz opened her door to find an unknown man with a bouquet of roses. He professed to be looking for another woman but finally gave the roses to her. One thing led to another, and soon they were married. The now Leonore Sutterlin was bringing home documents, some 3,000 of them, from her job at the West German Foreign Ministry. Heinz Sutterlin would photograph them and Leonore would then take them back to the Foreign Ministry. This lasted until 1967 when Heinz's spymaster boss, Colonel Evgeny Runge, defected and told all. This did not end well. Leonore had been madly in love with Heinz. When it came out at the trial that Heinz had been ordered to marry one of three secretaries and that she had been duped, she committed suicide.

6. SECRETARY TO FIVE WEST GERMAN PRESIDENTS

In 1987 one Margarete Hoeke, age 51, was convicted of spying for the KGB. This poor woman, who was described as a "gray mouse," had been secretary to five West German presidents. According to court documents, she had been spying for at least 11 years and probably much longer. She had taken a lipstick camera to work in the West German president's office where she had access to 1,700 secret documents. Intelligence people said she was "one of the most successful and best placed spies the KGB ever had in West Germany." She said she spied out of love for Franz Becker who seduced her in 1968. In this poor woman's confession in court, we see the prototype target of the Communist bloc intelligence services. She testified that she grew up feeling unloved by her family and that she was single and lonely in Bonn when approached by Becker. "I did whatever he wanted me to do. I didn't do it out of conviction. I had a bad conscience, but I just had the feeling that I simply had to be with him," she testified. As for Becker, he skedaddled, never to be seen again.

5. THE PROFESSOR HENRY HIGGINS OF WHORES

In *My Fair Lady*, Professor Higgins tried to uplift Eliza Doolittle, form her manners, and make her socially acceptable to her betters. Dr. Stephen Ward, a somewhat kinky London society osteopath, set himself a similar humanitarian mission with one Christine Keeler, among others. Dr. Ward taught his girls not only how to manage their manners but also how to lend a little excitement to the sexually jaded lives and sometimes perverse tastes of his moneyed, high-class friends—today, researchers would include U.S. President John Kennedy among those who sampled Ward's stable.

The story begins one day when the well-constructed Christine was swimming nude in the Astor family pool. The Secretary of State for War John Profumo happened to be present and as the report later said, "he was overcome with a desire for carnal knowledge of her." Soon the wish was the deed, but others, including a Soviet GRU officer named Yevgeny Ivanov, were also having these wishes and doing these deeds with Miss Keeler. This became a major public scandal. Profumo at first fibbed but then resigned. Ward was convicted on the trumped-up charge that he was living off prostitutes when surely it was they who were living off him. Convicted, he died of a fatal overdose of sleeping pills.

Only years later did MI-5's complicity in all this come out. Yes, they did feel terrible about leaving the good doctor out to dry. And yes, they had asked him to set up a honey trap for Ivanov to blackmail him into becoming an agent in place or defecting. Ward also played an unmentioned part in the back channel communications between Britain and the Kremlin during the Cuban Missile Crisis. Ward, it is now clear, was a real life victim of that old TV serial cliché warning to secret agents: "The secretary will disavow any knowledge of you." The titles of two later books on these sordid events tell much: *Honeytrap: The Secret Worlds of Stephen Ward* by Anthony Summers and Stephen Dorril and *An Affair of State: The Profumo Case and the Framing of Stephen Ward* by Phillip Knightly and Caroline Kennedy.

7. MAN ON MAN

One permutation of men as sexual bait to extract information from insiders is the use of homosexuals. The best examples are British, with the completely dissolute Guy Burgess leading the way. In the late 1930s, Burgess was sexually entangled with one Edouard Pfeiffer, a close friend of French Premier Edouard Daladier. With this connection, Burgess was able in 1938 and 1939 to pass on to MI-6 detailed accounts of meetings of the French Cabinet. This insider information, complete with descriptions of each cabinet member's stand on issues did wonders to boost Burgess's bona fides within British Intelligence and also undoubtedly within Soviet Intelligence. Burgess also told sordidly amusing tales of Pfeiffer's seduction of young boys. (Pfeiffer was an officer of the French Boy Scouts organization, which gave him much opportunity in this regard.) On one occasion, Burgess found Pfeiffer in full evening dress, playing Ping-Pong with a naked boy lying across the table substituting for the net. Another time, Burgess found himself in a male brothel in Paris as he and other high notables danced around a young naked boy tied to a post, whipping him. Burgess could seem to find the strangest bonding rituals.

8. GIVING "200 WOMEN THE BEST SEX EVER"

This is the tale of John Symonds, a onetime Scotland Yard detective who went bad and became a Romeo agent for the KGB. Actually, Mr. Symonds says that he went good with the help of two beautiful KGB women instructors who greatly improved his skills in the bedroom. It is not clear what information he gained from the 200 women he claimed he gave "the best sex ever," but it is clear that he spent 18 months in a British jail as one of his rewards.

9. AN INTELLIGENCE AGENCY NOT A LONELY HEARTS CLUB

Markus Wolf was the head of East German Foreign Intelligence Service who sent the Romeo spies westward. He describes and defends these efforts in his autobiography, *Man Without a Face*. One of his best agents in the West German government was Gabrielle (Gaby) Gast, the senior intelligence analyst in the Federal Intelligence Service concerned with the Soviet Union and Eastern Europe. Gast was an intelligent woman with a Ph.D. who had been raised in a conservative, middle-class home. In trying to make sense of how this none too handsome Romeo had seduced this Juliet and led her to espionage, Wolf offers this: "Rough and ready, he had a sort of proletarian charm that can be fatally attractive to sheltered middle-class women."

Wolf tried to save her from exposure by destroying her file when German unification became inevitable in the early 1990s, but another Stasi officer trying to save his own neck gave her away. As Markus Wolf wrote, defending these operations: "As long as there is espionage, there will be Romeos seducing unsuspecting Juliets with access to secrets. After all, I was running an intelligence agency, not a lonely hearts club."

10. ANOTHER PLAIN ONE

In his chapter on Romeo spies used to seduce West German women, Markus Wolf continually gives hope to plain men everywhere. In introducing us to "Roland G." Wolf writes: "It remains a mystery to me what it was about him that was so attractive to women, but there must have been something, because . . . he managed to persuade two highly placed and resourceful women to spy for us." In the case under discussion Roland was sent to the Alliance Française in Paris to mingle with the West German secretaries sent there to learn French. Here he bedded a young secretary, Gerda Osterrieder, who eventually was taking home bags of documents from Telco, the decoding center of the West German Foreign Office, to the delight of Roland G. and Mr. Wolf. Unfortunately, Gerda was transferred to Poland and rather than arouse suspicions by moving Roland, the Stasi allowed the separation. Gerda became lonely and began to drink heavily. In this condition, she confided her problems to a friendly journalist who turned out to be a West German Intelligence Officer. Roland made it out, barely in time. Gerda did prison time.

Cover Jobs

H ere we describe the cover jobs that agents use to cover what they really do—spy and run spies. These seem to be the jobs that give plausible explanation to lots of travel, odd hours, and curiosity. First the easy ones.

1. CLOAK AND STRIPED PANTS

This one is almost too easy, posing as a diplomat. The downside is that the opposition is aware of the trick. Defectors say that two-thirds of the personnel in a Russian embassy are intelligence officers, and the remaining third are informers and sources for the intelligence people, if they know what is good for them. This probably has not changed much since the end of the Cold War. On the American side, the intelligence people in an embassy are often kept at arm's length by the diplomatic staff and given titles that are transparent to almost anyone who takes the time to look around—Commercial Counselor, for example.

2. TRAVELING SALEMAN

This is also a favorite. British MI-6 supplied businessman Grenville Wynne with a mobile showroom, and he dutifully traipsed around Eastern Europe showing off his stock of goods. He was the contact for Oleg Penkovsky, and they were both caught. Penkovsky was executed. Wynne never really recovered from his harrowing experience of captivity in the Lubyanka Prison before being traded to freedom.

3. REPORTER

Journalism, of course, is perfect. Traveling and asking questions is the very core of journalism, so this is a very believable cover. Unfortunately, all intelligence agencies know this and suspect the other side's "journalists." The list here would be a long one. Kim Philby masqueraded as a journalist in the 1930s during the Spanish Civil War, while reporting to the Soviets. After he was pushed out of MI-6 in the early 1950s the intelligence people obtained for him a job reporting on the Mideast and doing some intelligence errands. He was still working for the Soviets and eventually ran away to Moscow.

4. DEALER IN RARE BOOKS

This has a good sound. If time is money then the ability to spend your time reading is a high-status use of it. Some of this prestige and patina of gentility rub off on the people who deal in books, particularly rare books, thus providing a good cover. Remember the Krogers nee Cohens in England. Peter Kroger's cover as a rare book dealer was never questioned until the British MI-5 trailed an agent right to his door.

5. PHOTOGRAPHER

Either as a profession or as a hobby, photography provides a good reason to have a camera and the chemicals for developing. You can have all the paraphernalia for microfilming documents. You can even make microdots with an ordinary camera and fine-grained black-and-white film straight from the camera store. Here is how you do it. Using the fine-grain black-and-white film, photograph the document with a normal lens. Develop and fix the negative normally, and dry it. Then take a piece of cardboard—the back of a legal pad is fine—cut out a piece the size of the negative and tape the negative across the opening. Stand this on a table with a lightbulb behind it. From the opposite side place your camera four feet away, and focus on the backlighted negative. A tripod would be nice, but a dictionary on the table will lift the camera high enough if you have mounted the negative low enough. Now take a picture of the negative from this distance. Develop the negative. That little dot on the negative is your microdot of the original letter. Put it under a microscope and read it. It's probably just as good as the work that Mrs. Cohen/Kroger was doing in England.

6. HIDING IN THE IVY

Another classic spy cover is the college professor. Not only do intelligence officers pose as professors, but the KGB and its Eastern Bloc friends were for many years most interested in recruiting professors with expertise in computing, business affairs, and defense, areas where the West was ahead. This could also be tricky for spies from a Communist culture. Karl Koecher, the KGB/Czech spy, tried to burrow into the American academic scene posturing as a virulent antiCommunist only to be let go because his philosophical stand offended the rest of the department. How many outsiders would understand that a large portion of American academia in the late 1960s and the 1970s was strongly anti-antiCommunist?

7. **AUTHOR**

Whereas newspaper writers and other journalists have a sort of temporary, maybe even sleazy feel to them, writers of serious books are viewed as more substantial people. This is another cover where the British have been in the vanguard. Before World War II, Section D of MI-6 sent an agent A. F. Rickman to Sweden to write a book on Sweden's iron ore. The fact that Rickman knew nothing of Sweden, Swedish, iron, or secret intelligence work was not then seen as an impediment. He wrote the book, thus taking on the mantle of expert, and began business importing machinery for the mining of said ore. Sometimes the books themselves can be of help. KGB officer Vladimir Merkulov, under cover as a diplomat in the Soviet Embassy in Copenhagen, used liberal amounts of cash to have an author launch a campaign to make Scandinavia a nuclear-free zone. During the 1950s and '60s, CIA agents wrote several books, including several Fodor's travel guides. Eugene Fodor was an old OSS man, so he was part of the club and was both willing and witting.

8. **GENTLEMAN**

Admittedly this one is going out of style and existence. Even in 1940, U.S. immigration authorities in New York were taken aback by the passport of one of Intrepid's agents, which listed his occupation as "Gentleman." Another "gentleman" who comes to mind was Major General Sir Stewart Menzies (pronounced Minn-giss). Who on the outside would have guessed that this clubbable member of the gentry, who spent his time fox hunting and pheasant shooting, was "C," the head of the British Secret Service?

9. INTOURIST GUIDE

Intourist was the official and thus only Soviet tourist agency. Western tourists needed guides in the Soviet Union and Intourist supplied them. Lots of the guides were KGB women on the lookout for lonely, high-ranking Western officials to seduce. Aeroflot, the Soviet airline, was pretty much the preserve of the GRU, Soviet military intelligence.

10. ALL THE RUSSIANS EMPLOYED BY WESTERN EMBASSIES IN MOSCOW

Where to start is the problem. There was hardly any employment job description filled by the Russians in the Western embassies that did not bag or bed its share of Western personnel from diplomats to guards. In 1988, when writer Ronald Kessler questioned the chief spokesman for the Soviet Foreign Ministry, Gennadi Gerasimov, about penetration of the U.S. Embassy, Gerasimov responded: "What do you mean penetration? Marines penetrated into our girls. This is real penetration. This was the real penetration. We didn't make a big fuss over it."

The Rich and Famous Worked Here, Too

1. NOEL COWARD

Even in the restrictive atmosphere of intelligence, Coward was irrepressible. He delighted in stamping over "Highly Confidential" on documents with his own stamp that said "Highly Truthful." There has long been a great deal of reluctance to admit that Coward worked for British Intelligence, but recently released documents suggest he was on board as early as 1938. He was probably in Section D of MI-6, where his good friend William Stephenson worked. Exactly what he did is the big question.

2. ALEXANDER KORDA (1893–1956)

Korda, a Hungarian of Jewish extraction, was a prominent movie producer of the 1930s, '40s, and '50s with such films as *The Lion Has Wings* and *That Hamilton Woman*. He was a full-blown British Intelligence agent in the United States during World War II, working to break down isolationism and involve the United States in the war. His offices both in California and in Rockefeller Center in New York were covers for British Intelligence operations. He was also a good friend of Sir William Stephenson (Intrepid), the head of British Intelligence in the United States. His work in the United States was so helpful that he was knighted during the war, which, given the prejudices of the time, baffled many in the British public. How could it be, they asked, that a divorced Hungarian Jew, who had not even been in England during the war, got knighted? In 1953 Korda, still close to British Intelligence, let his bank account be used to piggyback money from secret British government accounts to finance the intellectual magazine *Encounter,* which was being run by the CIA and British Intelligence as part of their front, the Congress for Cultural Freedom.

3.   JULIA SPIED HERE

Before she brought French cooking to the attention of the American public with her massive cookbook and TV show, Julia Child was a spy. Child, née Julia McWilliams, worked for OSS in China and Ceylon, now Sri Lanka. It was on these assignments that she met her husband. After the war, he was posted by the State Department to France. Julia was bowled over by the wonderful French food and the rest of the story is writ large in sauces.

4.   MOE THREW HERE

We are talking here of the Greek ideal—the disciplined, cultivated mind in the disciplined, trained body. Moe Berg, major league baseball player, Princeton graduate, linguist, and spy. He played catcher for a number of major league teams over a 16-year career. Moreover, baseball was a great cover. These were the days of barnstorming, where major league pick-up teams toured the United States and the world playing exhibition games against teams of local worthies—often doubling or tripling their major league salaries. On a 1934 barnstorming trip to Japan, Moe filmed Tokyo harbor

and the military installations along the coast. Tradition
has it that these films were later used for Jimmy Doolittle's raid on Tokyo after Pearl Harbor. In 1941 Berg
joined Nelson Rockefeller's South American intelligence operation, and in 1943 he joined OSS. His OSS
career included parachuting into Yugoslavia to evalu-
ate the partisans, and going into Norway and Switzerland. After the war, he worked for NATO. Tradition says
he continued his secret work for the rest of his life.

5. **WILLIAM F. BUCKLEY JR.**

WFB is the 6th of 10 children of a wealthy Texas oilman
who had moved to a Connecticut estate. There William
Buckley was raised by the Mexican household help so
that Spanish was his first language. This may seem surprising to those who have seen Mr. Buckley on American television, because his accent seems not Spanish
but faintly British. He did go to grade school in England, so that might be the answer. Before attending
college, he went into the military and after that went to
Yale. There political scientist Willmore Kendall recruited him for the CIA. (Once again—the CIA/Yale
connection.) Buckley's brief time in the Agency was
spent in Mexico where he put his Spanish fluency to
work editing the onetime Peruvian Communist Eudocio
Ravines's book *The Road to Yenan*, which detailed the
Communist quest for world domination.

6. **MARLENE SANG FOR THE OSS**

As part of its psychological warfare against the Germans, the OSS had sexy songstress Marlene Dietrich
record sentimental popular songs in German such as
"I'll Get By," "I Couldn't Sleep a Wink Last Night," and
"Lili Marlene." These nice translations sung by the
wonderful Marlene were not just to help the Wehrmacht
wile away the hours, but to make the German troops

feel homesick and depressed. This "Musak" project was the entertainment part of the "Soldatensender West" radio programs. The political side of these shows was the province of the marvelously devious Sefton Delmer, whom we have met elsewhere. After the war, Dietrich received America's highest civilian medal, the Medal of Freedom, and France made her a Knight of the Legion of Honor. According to Elizabeth P. McIntosh in her book *Sisterhood of Spies: The Women of the OSS*, Bill Donovan even helped Dietrich retrieve the rights to these recordings, and they were issued commercially in 1951.

7. GOLDBERG AND THE OSS

Arthur Goldberg is well known for his work as a Supreme Court justice and as American ambassador to the United Nations. Less well known is his work as head of the Labor Desk of OSS. Goldberg's job was to make connections with the discontented labor unions in Hitler's Fortress Europe. He felt that the labor movement in Europe, even in Germany, was strongly anti-Hitler and would make the basis for both subverting the Third Reich and for supplying information on German production and supply problems. Goldberg convinced William Donovan, head of OSS, and Donovan sent him to New York to work with Allen Dulles and the British in Rockefeller Center.

8. "DOUBTLESS SHE WAS EXPERT BETWEEN THE SHEETS"

These are the words *The Economist* used in her obituary when exploring the reasons that Pamela Digby Churchill Heywood Harriman had climbed as high as she had in life. After all, she ended being appointed by Bill Clinton as American ambassador to France. Early in World War II, she had married Randolf, the son of British Prime Minister Winston Churchill. She bore Randolf a son and with her husband away at war, quickly turned to other matters, which included a succession of lovers. One of these was U.S. President Franklin Roosevelt's personal representative, Averell Harriman. Apparently Max Beaverbrook, adviser to Winston Churchill, was ecstatic at the conquest. Harriman had not been on British soil 24 hours and already he was compromised. The British now had a direct pipeline into Harriman's bedroom.

9. EUGENE FODOR, THE TRAVEL GUIDE MAN

During World War II, Fodor worked for Bill Donovan's OSS. Fodor stayed close to intelligence work, and during the Cold War several agents "covered" themselves by writing his guidebooks. Fodor told the *New York Times* that the agents "were all highly professional, high quality. We never let politics be smuggled into the books."

10. NELSON ALDRICH ROCKEFELLER

A number of the Rockefeller and Aldrich cousins were useful to World War II intelligence operations, none more so than Nelson, later to be governor of New York State and vice president of the United States. For starters, Nelson was in charge of renting Rockefeller Center, so it was he that gave Intrepid's British Security Coordination two floors of space for a phennig rent. Similar arrangements were made for British Intelligence fronts such as Fight for Freedom, which demanded an immediate declaration of war on Germany. But this was only for starters. In the summer of 1940, President Roosevelt appointed Nelson "Coordinator of Inter-American affairs," an intelligence outfit masquerading as a cultural outreach organization for Latin America.

Favorite Watering Holes—A Tour of Western Europe and the United States

S pies like to unwind and have a drink now and then just like other people—maybe more so. It's a stressful business.

1. FRAUNCES TAVERN—MANHATTAN, NEW YORK

Although he used many taverns during his days as spymaster, General George Washington spent one of his most satisfying nights here at Fraunces. (Yes, George drank, or at least he sent Congress some hefty liquor bills to be paid.) The day before, the British had evacuated New York. The war was won, and George spent the night here and forayed out to pay off his spy network—editor James Rivington, Culper Jr., and the whole crew that made his victories possible.

2. IN GERMANY IN THE 1960s

A note from a friendly spy stationed in Germany in the 1960s says: "In the '60s anyplace within five blocks of the I. G. FARBAN building in Berlin would qualify. The hottest place on a Friday afternoon/night would be the Officers Club—a lot of chatter there. Perhaps the Seppllehaller."

3. A CIA FAVORITE—EVAnS FARM Inn

The address was 1696 Chain Bridge Road, McLean, Virginia. This was a favorite with Agency people because it was so close to CIA headquarters. Spies even met their agents here (which sounds bizarre to me). The setting was so picturesque that some had their weddings on the grounds. Alas, it is now closed and has been subdivided into lots with huge, expensive homes. I am told that the exploding property values and taxes in the burgeoning neighborhood simply became too much.

4. TWO I. W. HARPERS AnD A 15 PERCEnT TIP

In the days when he led his luncheon group here at La Nicoise at 1721 Wisconsin Avenue, NW, James Jesus Angleton (give the "Jesus" the Spanish pronunciation), head of CIA counterintelligence, ate great helpings of seafood and had a couple of drinks at table 41—always the same seat. With its mirror, he could see the whole room.

5. WHITE'S, 37 ST. JAMES'S STREET, London

This is London's oldest (1693) and certainly one of its most prestigious clubs. The World War II head of MI-6, Stewart Menzies, used White's as an annex to his office on Broadway. He is said to have interviewed recruits here and "held court in the bar." Author Anthony Cave Brown tells us that supplies of German wines like Hine '28 and Wolfschmidt Kumnmel never ran out at White's, even during the war. Brown also says that

Menzies had "his most secret (or most ticklish) mail sent . . . [to White's] in the belief that it was more likely to be safe in the hands of Groom, the hall porter than the mail room of the secret service."

6. BOODLES, 28 ST. JAMES'S STREET, LONDON

If Menzies, the head of British Secret Intelligence, did business at White's, then his assistants such as "Uncle" Claude Dansey belonged to Boodles just down St. James Street. Ian Fleming, assistant to the head of Naval Intelligence, was a member. Readers of his James Bond novels have had Boodles well described to them. Fleming calls it "Blade's" and his spymaster "M" spends his off-hours there.

7. HAY-ADAMS HOTEL BAR, 16TH & H STREETS, NW, WASHINGTON, D.C.

It was in the bar here at the plush Hay-Adams (on the site of the houses of Secretary of State John Hay and the author/statesman Henry Adams) that Oliver North wined and dined and lobbied potential angels for his Iran-Contra schemes. Hay-Adams is so convenient—it is just across Lafayette Square from the Old Executive Office Building where Ollie and the lovely Fawn Hall shredded documents.

8. THE PENTHOUSE AT BRATENAHL PLACE, A PLUSH ENCLAVE TUCKED BETWEEN CLEVELAND AND LAKE ERIE

Of all the places that the Northern Ohio Chapter of AFIO (Association of Former Intelligence Officers) meets to search for the meaning of life, this is my favorite. I am taking these notes while looking across the room at 30 or so intelligence veterans clinking glasses and schmoozing in the Penthouse at Bratenahl Place. The view down the shoreline and the cityscape is wonderful. Cleveland and its environs have such a rich espionage history. It is only an hour by air from Washington. There is a large ethnic population, so a foreign accent raises no notice. The secret negotiations to end the Vietnam War started within sight of here.

9. THE STORK CLUB, NEW YORK CITY

The Stork Club is now gone. A small park occupies the site of Sherman Billingsley's hot spot of the 1930s, '40s, and '50s. It even had its own television show in the 1950s. Sir William Stephenson (Intrepid) schmoozed with everyone useful to British Intelligence here— Helen Rogers Reid, who ran the *New York Herald Tribune*, journalist Dorothy Thompson, and many others. One of his favorite journalists, Walter Winchell, had a table here; J. Edgar Hoover, the FBI head, would stop in on trips to New York. Stephenson's staff also frequented the Stork Club. Ernest Cuneo and his future wife, a member of Intrepid's staff, are pictured in my book *Desperate Deception* at a table at the Stork Club.

10. THE CHOP HOUSE OVERLOOKING THE SKATING RINK AT ROCKEFELLER CENTER, NEW YORK CITY

Since the Rockefellers (Nelson, later vice president of the United States, was in charge of rentals) thoughtfully gave British Intelligence two floors for a "phennig rent," the chop house was close to the office and several British Intelligence agents remember being recruited or meeting here. In his book *Cloak and Gown,* Professor Robin Winks of Yale tells us of Yale man Donald Downes. "Downes was eager to be recruited, and when he met with a 'Mr. Howard'—in fact Colonel Charles

Howard 'Dick' Ellis, a top British secret agent . . . at a chophouse looking out on the skating rink at Rockefeller Plaza, he agreed to spy on his fellow Americans to see whether Nazi money was supporting isolationist groups."

Bosses (Spymasters)

The great ones, as in most professions, are natu-rals—people born devious or raised to it from an early age. People who believe that honesty is not al-ways the best policy, but that it may occasionally be an interesting strategy—people who love the great game for itself. And none was more in love with it than MI-6's "Uncle" Claude Dansey.

1. UNCLE CLAUDE HAD QUILLS

Lieutenant Colonel Sir Claude Edward Majorbanks Dansey was a man utterly unknown to the public and even to specialists during his lifetime. As intelligence historian Anthony Cave Brown has written of Dansey, he was "a man who could commit murder easily, so long as he was not caught—in short a man capable of anything, and therefore exactly the sort who could rise to great heights in the secret service . . ." "Claude Dansey was an utter shit," said former intelligence man and later Regis professor of history at Oxford, Hugh Trevor-Roper, ". . . corrupt, incompetent, but with a certain low cunning." Given the snobbery and arro-gance of the Oxford professorate, these snippy com-

133

ments are a sure tip-off that "Uncle Claude" had gotten the best of the good professor. Other compatriots have similarly testified that Dansey possessed the qualities of a great spymaster . . . "an utter snake," ". . . the only truly evil man I have ever met," they said. This is high praise indeed for an intelligence chief.

Dansey spent over half a century consumed by intelligence operations from Africa to America to Europe. As Colonel Z, he created a 1930s European intelligence network, the "Z Network," parallel to but separate from MI-6. His biographers credit him with creating the Lucy Ring in Switzerland as a way to feed the Soviets information from the broken Enigma ciphers without telling them about the breaking of the cipher. If that were true, it would explain why John Cairncross's FBI file is still so secret, since Cairncross would have been in on such a tricky and delicate operation. It would also explain why Cairncross was never prosecuted for being a Soviet spy. At any rate Dansey was knighted immediately after information passed on by the Lucy Ring gave the Soviets a victory at Kursk, history's largest tank battle and one that destroyed the German Army's offensive abilities on the Eastern Front.

That was not all for such a gifted intelligence man. The French made him commander of the Legion of Honor; the Belgians gave him the Chevalier of the Order of Leopold and the United States gave him the Legion of Merit. "Uncle Claude" actually came from a long line of British spymasters, certainly going back to Queen Elizabeth's Sir Francis Walsingham.

2. **BY APPOINTMENT TO HER MAJESTY THE QUEEN**

The Queen was Elizabeth I and never did a monarch have a more devoted spymaster than Sir Francis Walsingham. The realm's intelligence needs were great, what with Catholic plots and everything. Elizabeth I was a cheapskate, and Walsingham spent his own vast fortune and was deeply in debt when he died in 1590. Picture the head of the FBI or CIA doing that today. Let's look at what Elizabeth got for *his* money. Walsingham despised Catholics.

When the Catholic Mary Stuart, Queen of Scots, fled to England in 1568, Elizabeth imprisoned her. Since Mary was the hope of English Catholics, Walsingham made it his business to infiltrate her entourage, intercept her mail, decode the secret messages of her Catholic supporters, and, to increase the fun, introduce his own letters into that correspondence. Thus, he discovered the "Babington Plot" to assassinate Elizabeth and put the Catholic Mary on the throne.

Encouraged by the prisoner interview techniques common in that age, some confessed and a number went to the block. Walsingham used the "decoded messages" from Mary to get Elizabeth to sign Mary's death warrant. To this day, ugly words like "forgery" dot the scholarly discussions of Sir Walsingham's evidence. Mary went to the chopping block in February 1587 calmly denying that she wrote the messages.

3. IT'S "UNCLE MAX," BOYS AND GIRLS

Another strange bird in the intelligence aviary was Maxwell Knight. To millions of children who listened to his weekly nature broadcasts on the BBC he was "Uncle Max." In addition, he certainly did love nature, as his succession of exotic animal pets and books on nature attested. (One of the books was illustrated by spy novelist David Cornwell—John le Carré.) On the job as an MI-5 agent runner, he was "Captain King" or

"M." Women loved him and he ran them as agents very well. He used Joan Gray (Miss X) to break the Woolrich Arsenal spy case in 1938. He used Joan Miller in May 1940, to arrest Tyler Kent, the U.S. Embassy code clerk who threatened to make the very secret Roosevelt/Churchill correspondence public. Exposure would have threatened the carefully orchestrated effort to bring the United States into World War II. Although women loved him, and he married three of them and had several live-ins, he also puzzled them since he never had sex with any of them. There was a slight scandal when wife number one committed suicide. On the other hand, Knight disliked Sir Anthony Blunt, also a homosexual, and Blunt always kept a wary eye on Knight.

4. THIS BOY SCOUT WAS NO BOY SCOUT

The term *Boy Scout* has come to have the connotation of an innocent, straight arrow. How this came to be would certainly be an interesting story. Certainly, the creator of the Boy Scouts, Lord Robert Baden-Powell (1857–1941), was anything but an innocent. He was a devious, conniving, major player at the great game of espionage. Baden-Powell did so well on the preliminary examination upon entering the army that he was excused from further basic training and commissioned immediately in the 13th Hussars. Over the next few years he saw India, South Africa, and Malta. By the 1890s, when he was appointed as an intelligence officer for the Mediterranean, he was a veteran of both warfare and intelligence. The Mediterranean assignment was perfect for him.

To spy on the fortress of Cattaro in Dalmatia in the Austro-Hungarian Empire, Baden-Powell dressed as a nearsighted lepidopterist, complete with butterfly net and sketchbook. He sketched the plan of the fortress into the wings of his butterfly drawings. On another occasion, he passed himself off as a fly fisherman and amateur painter to discover which valleys in a certain country could be used to move troops. The troops on maneuvers in those valleys even gave him cigarettes and coffee. Of course, he wrote a complete report on their guns, equipment, and conversations. He watched the secret testing of a new machine gun as a booze-soaked, stumbling drunk. On a trip down the Danube to check the fortifications, he used a whole series of ruses—bad rudder, time out to fish (he was really taking soundings)—one lie after another. In fact, his life before World War I seems a series of disguises, lies, and fakery. As one book says of him: "Beyond question [he was] one of the most gifted secret service agents that ever lived." As I said, hardly a Boy Scout.

5. RAFAEL "RAFI" EITAN—THE EICHMAnn SnATCHER

Eitan is the very personification of Israeli Intelligence's utterly cold-blooded ruthlessness and meticulous planning. "Rafi," the Mossad's longtime deputy director of operations, made his reputation by both engineering and personally assisting in the Mossad's 1960 kidnapping of Nazi Adolf Eichmann, who had sent millions of Jews to the death camps. The capture took two years of work and planning after Eichmann was first spotted living near Buenos Aires, Argentina. The Mossad bought a small long-range airliner just for the trip.

The cover story was that the passengers were supposed to be a delegation sent to celebrate 150 years of Argentinean independence. Rafi rented half a dozen safe houses and several cars, and he was right there in the car directing the snatch of Eichmann from a city street. Eichmann was spirited back to Israel with the delegation, tried, and executed.

Actually, he had more of a delay and more of the niceties than many other Nazis received right after the war. Israel was poor and just getting started after the war and could not afford the airplanes and planning that went into the Eichmann capture. "Nokmin," or avengers, simply executed Nazi criminals where they found them—not very nice, but very cheap. This also supplied the Mossad a whole generation of experienced assassins, who seem to have carefully passed their skills along, if I read the newspapers correctly.

6. THE CLASSIC SPYMASTER *CUM* OPERATIVE

Wilhelm Stieber, a Berlin lawyer, was another natural spy and a fundamental cog in Otto von Bismarck's successful effort to grab territory and create the German state you recognize today. Bismarck commissioned Stieber and gave him a little over half a million dollars in today's money to find out everything he could about the Austrian army. Using what today would be called "commercial cover," Stieber spent several months traveling around Austrian military camps as an itinerant peddler. He and his wagon of goods were welcomed everywhere. He seemed good for morale. From one side of the wagon he sold religious statues; from the other side he sold pornography. He was very popular with the troops.

He and his inside dope were even more popular
with Bismarck. It gave the Germans that extra edge in
battle. The Battle of Sadowa ended the Austro-Prussian
War of 1866 in only seven weeks. This knocked Austria
out of German affairs. Next up was France. Stieber employed some 15,000 agents; he was an open-minded
man who used all strata of society—barmaids, prostitutes, servants, peddlers, convicts, smugglers, forgers,
retired military officers, and such. (The order the CIA
got a few years ago not to hire any agents with criminal
records certainly would have gotten a hoot from
Stieber.) They reported on everything from bridges and
fortifications to the loyalties of local leaders and politicians. Stieber was a pioneer. He was the first spymaster
to use swarms of agents throughout an enemy country.
The Franco-Prussian War of 1870 was over quickly,
and in 1871 the Germans used the Palace of Versailles
(about 14 miles from Paris) to crown the German em-
peror. Bismarck is in the painting of the ceremony in a
nice white outfit. Stieber got a medal.

7.   **"WILD BILL" DONOVAN**

One day during World War I, Major William Donovan
led his men on a three-mile run, jumping over walls,
leaping streams, crawling under barbed wire. At the
end, his men lay exhausted and panting. Donovan
glared at them, yelling that he was carrying the same
50-pound pack, he was 10 years older, and he felt fine.
From the back of the group came the cry: "But we ain't
as wild as you, Bill." The name would stick with him
the rest of his life. William Donovan is another of those
originals who might well not make it past the vetting in
these blander times. Donovan loved war and action; it
is doubtful that any service today would allow its head

to sneak behind enemy lines in Burma or put himself so close to the front in Europe. However, Donovan's energy and imagination were certainly indispensable to starting the COI/OSS.

8. LITTLE BILL STEPHENSON—"INTREPID"

We know that Bill Stephenson came to the United States in 1940 to represent a myriad of British Intelligence organizations and to push the United States into the war. It is now becoming clear that a full examination may be in order. The clearest fact about William Stephenson comes from a Canadian book, *The True Intrepid*, by Bill Macdonald. Much of what we thought we knew about "Intrepid's" life turns out to be what the pros would call a legend—a phony biography. So once again, we have the self-selection of spies—people who are naturally devious pursuing the trade most in need of the skill.

9. THE MAN WITHOUT A FACE—MARKUS WOLF

As amazing as it might seem, it was almost 20 years after he took control of East Germany's Foreign Intelligence Service before Western intelligence services had any idea what Wolf looked like. He had even landed in the United States (accidentally, when his Russian plane ran out of fuel on a Moscow to Cuba trip) without being identified. His memoirs—*Man without a Face*—are a great read. He takes you along as he plants sleeper agents, reveals how one of his agents brought down West German chancellor Willie Brandt, and how he sent forth Romeo agents to conquer the bedrooms of the West. This may have been a little tough on the targets but he writes: "I was running an intelligence service, not a lonely hearts club."

10. THE GREAT WHITE CASE OFFICER—ALLEN DULLES

When he was head of the CIA Allen Dulles left most of
the day-to-day operations to his talented subordinates,
while he spent much of his time looking over secret
operations, as a case officer would, hence his nickname at the Agency, "The Great White Case Officer."

The Price Is Right

I t is very true, that it is possible that a case may happen, that a man may serve his country by a bribe well placed, or an intrigue of pleasure with a woman." So wrote John Adams, diplomat and second president of the United States. This quote certainly does not fit with Adams's rather proper, prim modern reputation, but he lived at a very tough time and he did much of his diplomatic dealing in the very cosmopolitan environs of Europe.

An acquaintance of mine, long influential in the higher areas of the CIA, thinks my use of the word "bribe," unduly harsh. He also suggested that both British MI-6 and the CIA would be unhappy to see this word used to describe their activities. A better word, my acquaintance suggested, might be "honorarium." This advice makes me feel much better. I for one would feel much better delivering an "honorarium" to a foreign official. The British term for an "honorarium" is "King George's Cavalry." As in, if all else fails, pay them; send in "King George's Cavalry."

1. CHEAP AT TWICE THE PRICE
Scholars have spilled much ink discussing how and why it was that Spain, a Fascist country, did not get

into World War II on the side of Germany. Nor did the Spanish invite the Germans to cross Spain to attack the British fortress Rock of Gibraltar. Hitler's discussions of these issues with General Franco were so unproductive that he said he would rather have all his teeth pulled than go through them again. Such ingratitude. Hitler had supplied Franco with planes, men, and supplies in the 1930s during the Spanish Civil War. The Soviets, of course, also gave similar goods to the Republican side. It turns out that British Intelligence gave the top Spanish generals "honorara" of between $1 million and $10 million 1940 dollars (between $10 million and $100 million in 2003 dollars). For this the Spanish generals had to do nothing and make sure they did nothing to help Hitler. They simply had to council General Franco to do nothing. Good work if it comes your way.

2. *AUFWANDSENTSCHADIGUNGEN* AND THE "BOHEMIAN CORPORAL"

Hitler never did sit well with most of his generals, those conservative people with "von" in their names. He was not of their class and he threatened, nay promised, to upset Germany's social structure by opening up the society. Is it any wonder that Field Marshal von Runstedt derisively called Hitler the "Bohemian corporal"? How to get his aristocratic generals to do what they were told until the Hitler Youth could come of age and replace them was the question on der Fuhrer's mind. His answer—bribe them. He had given this idea some satisfying test runs on the Reich Ministers in the 1930s but really started passing out the Reich Marks in the summer of 1940. The term *bribe* was, of course, too crass so the generals received *Aufwandsentschadigungen*, or "compensation for expenses." These were totally secret tax-exempt payments to the accounts of top military men and they were in addition to their regular salaries. Field Marshal level men received RM 4,000 per month; officers at the level of army generals received RM 2,000 per month.

Of all the reasons given in textbooks for the German officer corps getting along by going along and closing their eyes to many of the distasteful orders from the Nazis, bribery is seldom mentioned. Hitler also handed out some choice estates for the same purpose. Toward the end of the war Hitler seems to have become disillusioned with his efforts at bribery. He belatedly recognized that Stalin's solution of shooting the Soviet generals in the late 1930s had, in the long run, been better for discipline.

3. KERMIT ROOSEVELT'S PHALLUS

CIA man Kermit Roosevelt, the grandson of President Theodore Roosevelt, did much fine work to drive out Mossadeq and return the shah to full power in Iran in 1953. He did many other things, too. One of them was to deliver a $12 million . . . honorarium to General Naguib, who had been one of Nasser's associates in the overthrow of King Farouk in Egypt. When he found out about this payment Nasser forced General Naguib out of the government and made him cough up the $12 million. To prove to the West that he and his government could not be bribed, Nasser built something totally useless, the Cairo Tower known since then variously as "The CIA Monument," "Kermit Roosevelt's Erection" and "Kermit Roosevelt's Phallus."

4. DOING THE CONGO

In those nosy Congressional Pike Committee hearings of the 1970s it was revealed that the CIA had paid an unnamed African leader a million dollars over a 14-year period (equivalent to about $5 million in 2003 money). These dollars had paved the way for some successful CIA paramilitary operations in Africa in the 1960s. The prime candidate for this honor seems to be President Mobutu Sese Seko who fits the description largely because he was one of the few African leaders to survive for 14 years.

5. BUY THEM ALL

In January 1915 the British were desperately trying to hunt down the German ship *Dresden* off the coast of Chile. All those tough moral dilemmas—the First Sea Lord does not dismiss them; he never even considers them, in his note to the First Lord of the Admiralty Winston Churchill: "If our Minister to Chile [Francis Strange] had been worth his salt he would have bought up all the telegraph people." For his sensitive moral reservations in a wartime crisis the First Sea Lord labels Minister Strange "effete" and a "bloody fool." So much for that sense of British understatement.

6. BRIBERY BY THE NUMBERS

Some countries are more open to bribery than others. These are often countries that have fallen on hard times. This, of course, is a perfect description of present-day Russia. Two authors obviously dedicated to the public's right to know, Ryurik Povileiko and Ivan Stepanov, published a guide fittingly called *Bribe* that has a helpful fee schedule. My interest in academia was naturally sharpened by entries such as: "100 rubles (or a bottle of Ararat Cognac) for a teacher of a difficult subject and 1,000 rubles (or a crate of champagne) for a dean or a store manager." Those with higher aspirations will find that a company director or a government minister will cost a well-located Moscow apartment with two bathrooms. A state leader will cost upward of 10 million rubles, which should be discreetly deposited in a Swiss bank.

7. ON THE GENTLE ART OF BRIBERY

In his memoir *The Infernal Grove*, British Intelligence agent Malcolm Muggeridge tells us a number of important things about bribery as part of espionage. He mentions that when Americans arrived at his post they simply raised the "accepted tariff of bribes to astronomical proportions." He notes that bribery is an artform: "I found that bribery which inevitably played a large part in my Lourenco Marques activities, had as many subtleties and diversities as seduction. Thus, in certain circumstances, the passing of money had to be engineered in such a way that it seemed to happen of itself, which, in seduction terms, was the equivalent of lolling or reaching out an arm as though by accident."

8. IS THAT A "GRASS EATER" I SEE?

A "grass eater" in police terms is an officer who takes reasonable, gentlemanly bribes, who is judicious in his tastes and not greedy. (Greedy cops with unlimited desires for bribes are called "meat eaters.") In his book *Veil*, Bob Woodward describes how Eugenia Charles, the wildly pro-American prime minister of the tiny Caribbean island of Dominica, was given $100,000 by the CIA for asking the United States to invade Grenada. This, of course, helped to legitimize the invasion. If true, this has to be the best deal since the Dutch swapped some beads for Manhattan Island.

9. PISHKESH

In some cultures, some types of bribes are not considered illegal. The word *pishkesh* is Farsi (the language of Iran) for a "gift" given not for consideration but in the hope of a return at some time in the future.

10. OTHERS

Governments are leery about exposing their bribery to public view. Bribes are either kept secret or called something else, like "foreign aid." One secret is the great cost, whatever it was, to get the East German Stasi files on 1,000 CDs. Markus Wolf, the onetime head of the Stasi Foreign Intelligence section, says this was the greatest intelligence haul of all time. What sort of a bribe did this take and to whom was it paid? Wolf suggests that some Stasi official may have avoided prosecution in return for the CDs. In the outside world this is called bribery, but it is a common tool in the legal system with those who have the power to prosecute.

Freedom of the Press, for All Those Who Own a Press

In September 1941, Assistant Secretary of State Adolph Berle (rhymes with surly), wrote a note to another assistant secretary and buddy of President Franklin Roosevelt, Sumner Welles: "When they [British Intelligence] work up such an incident they apparently use the *New York Tribune* as a means of publication, much the same as they used to use the *Providence Journal* in the World War [World War I]." The British used both of these papers, of course, and a number of others to project their message that the United States should give the British money and get into both world wars. The phrase used was "The United States should accept its responsibilities as a World Power." British efforts to involve the United States in World War I and World War II involved finding sympathetic American publishers who would allow the British to plant their people in strategic newsroom positions or to plant material at will.

One secret British report on the newspaper operation said of friendly American publishers: "There is no need to list them all, but among those who rendered

service of particular value were George Backer, publisher of the *New York Post*, Ralph Ingersoll, editor of
PM, Helen Rogers Reid, who controls the *New York Herald Tribune*, Paul Patterson, publisher of the *Baltimore
Sun*, A. H. Sulzberger, President of the *New York
Times*, Walter Lippmann and several columnists, William Shirer, the commentator, and Walter Lemmon,
owner of station WRUL." During the Cold War, the
Americans, with their cash, took the British model to
its logical conclusion and bought interests in various
English-language newspapers and news organizations.
English-language papers and news services were fa-
vored because it was easier to dream up reasons for
American ownership and easier to place CIA people as
editors and reporters. These papers were both great
agent cover and great vehicles for propaganda. The
word is that at one time or another the CIA owned or
had an agent in at least one paper in every major foreign nonCommunist capital.

1. *THE PROVIDENCE JOURNAL* AND THE MINISTER WITHOUT PORTFOLIO

Adolph Berle was right, of course, in his note to FDR's
friend Sumner Welles. In the Roosevelt Library at Hyde
Park is a note saying that three of the *Providence
Journal*'s directors met in Washington at the British
Embassy and were guaranteed that funds had been al-
located to cover any losses the paper might suffer for
carrying British propaganda or other activities. One of
these directors was also the *Providence Journal*'s editor
and general manager, John R. Rathom—a man with, as
they say, a murky past. Rathom was born in the British
Empire and educated at one of Britain's most prestigious "public schools" (which are actually private),

Harrow. Even the *Journal* official history states: ". . . Rathom and the *Journal* went to war in earnest on the side of Britain and her allies, with the apparent purpose of getting the United States and a reluctant President Wilson conditioned for war."

The *Journal* and Rathom got the credit for all the scoops passed on to them by British Intelligence and its network of Czech agents (the Czechs wanted to destroy the Austro-Hungarian Empire, Germany's ally, so they could form their own country). Thus given legitimacy, the items were then passed to New York papers like the *New York Times* and even syndicated nationally before publication with the lead: "The *Providence Journal* will say this morning. . . ." However, Rathom and the *Journal* went far beyond being mere conduits for British propaganda; he and several staff members became part of British covert action. They stole the briefcase of Dr. Heinrich Albert, the paymaster for German secret operations in the United States, and handed it over to British Intelligence. Copies of papers in the briefcase were then passed to the White House. The *Providence Journal* people staged a drunken fight on the train in front of Dr. Albert. When he stood to watch the fight the *Providence Journal*'s Charles Stark reached over the seat and substituted an exact copy of Dr. Albert's briefcase, filled with old newspapers.

This little tale rarely makes the standard history books; the most recent rendering I have seen said that "Dr. Albert lost his briefcase." The results of this were wonderful for the British cause. The *Journal* eventually published a damning series on German Intelligence activities in the United States. President Wilson and assistants were greatly irritated at the Germans. Subsequent revelations included a scheme to involve Mexico in war against the United States and a plan to sink an ocean liner in New York Harbor when the entire U.S. fleet was in the East River for a grand review by President Wilson.

2. WHAT TIME IS GREENWICH?

The British (as their own secret history of World War II intelligence admits) pretty much had the run of the *New York Herald Tribune* on the eve of America's entry into World War II. Another such paper was *Greenwich Time* of Greenwich, Connecticut. Please note that is *Greenwich Time* and not *Times*. The name is a play on Greenwich Mean Time and the paper did numerous plays on this theme. As World War II approached it was clear that, though the ploy of using a newspaper to give credibility to bald-faced propaganda had been a dynamite success for the last war, the *Providence (R.I.) Journal's* cover was blown. For one thing, Rathom loved the spotlight and he had bragged about his exploits at every opportunity after World War I. Another vehicle was needed.

Stephan O. Metcalf, the owner and longtime president of the *Providence Journal,* quietly purchased the Greenwich, Connecticut, paper. Not so strangely, all but the legal minimum paperwork on this transaction has disappeared, but the results are clear. One Wythe Williams was brought in to edit *Greenwich Time.* In keeping with the "time" theme, Williams's column was called, "As the Clock Strikes." He also had a checkered past. Williams's FBI file 65-16107 runs to hundreds of pages and the prefix number, 65, suggests the Bureau was looking at him on "Espionage" matters. John Edgar Hoover never let people like this out of his sight. He always wanted to know where the bodies were buried. The FBI report says "Williams claims to have 'pipe lines' to Europe and his own news gatherers over there who smuggle data to him by use of codes and other unexplained and mysterious ways." This sounds like the explanations given for the material British Intelligence was feeding the *Providence Journal* in World War I. This "dogged reporting legwork," soon brought even greater rewards. By early 1940, Williams had his own radio show on station WOR, Mutual Broadcasting System, New York City. Williams played the British propaganda themes that the Western Hemisphere was in danger; the Germans were going to sabotage munitions plants; "Hitler was scheming the destruction of the Picatinny and Lake Denmark Arsenals in New Jersey." FBI agents reported to J. Edgar Hoover that Williams was "absolutely unreliable." Of course, as Mr. Williams's career illustrates, this need not be an impediment to a successful life in journalism.

3. *THE NEW YORK HERALD TRIBUNE* AND BRITISH INTELLIGENCE—LET ME COUNT THE WAYS

The secret British Security Coordination history of British Intelligence operations in World War II mentions five American newspaper owners as having "rendered service of particular value." Of the five newspapers, certainly the most useful vehicle for British Intelligence was the *New York Herald Tribune*. The Brits were plugged in so many different ways and the *Tribune* was part of so many different British Intelligence capers that the exact trail for many of these ploys may never be untangled until Soviet Intelligence opens its archives.

First, there was Helen Rogers Reid, the wife of the owner, Ogden Reid. Mrs. Reid was a strong personality; she had lived in England between 1905 and 1911 when

her future father-in-law, Whitelaw Reid, had been
American ambassador to Great Britain. She had been
his wife's social secretary. The Reids were family
friends of Stewart Menzies, the head of British MI-6.
Second, there were prominent *Tribune* columnists like
Walter Lippmann and Dorothy Thompson who were
important enough to be messaged independently by
the Brits. (Lippmann's brother-in-law, "Ivor" Bryce,
worked for British Intelligence and there are, among
Lippmann's papers at Yale, letters from Bryce concerning matters BSC wanted planted in the press.) One
project that few have ever tied together was the nomination of Wendell Willkie as the Republican candidate
in 1940. Willkie was a favorite of Mrs. Reid's and a favorite bed partner of her close friend and editor of the
Tribune's "Books" section, Irita Van Doren, Carl Van
Doren's ex-wife. Willkie was a lifelong Democrat, a
member of Tammany Hall, the Democratic machine in
New York City. A man who had never held office, he
was nominated by the Republicans for president. The
convention had turned down the preconvention favorites, all isolationists—Robert Taft, Arthur Vandenberg,
and Tom Dewey. All the friends of British Intelligence
were greatly relieved that the voter would have two in-
terventionists to choose from. It would be left to the
dazed Republican Convention witnesses to write titles
like "Who Doped the Elephant," and the "Miracle in
Philadelphia."

4. *THE BALTIMORE SUN*—ANOTHER BRIGHT SPOT IN THE BRITISH GALAXY OF HELPMATES

The BSC secret history tells us that the *Baltimore Sun*'s
publisher Paul Patterson rendered British Intelligence
great service. A member of the *Sun*'s board of direc-

tors, the curmudgeonly journalist H. L. Mencken, whose papers are now open, reiterates this. Mencken had stopped writing for the *Sun* in early 1941 when he became disgusted by the paper's bias. He wrote in his diary: "From the first to the last they were official organs and nothing more, and taking one day with another they were official organs of England rather than of the United States."

How did this happen? One day in March 1944, Patterson "dropped in" on Mencken for their "long delayed palaver." "I told Patterson that, in my judgment, the English had found him an easy mark, and made a monkey out of him. He . . . did not attempt to dispute the main fact. In the course of his talk I gathered . . . that he is entertained while in London by an Englishwoman who is the head of one of the women's auxiliary organizations—perhaps characteristically, he did not know its name. He also let fall the proud fact that she is a countess." Without doubt the woman was a granddaughter of Queen Victoria—Princess Alice, Countess of Athlone, commandant in chief of FANY, the First Aid Nursing Yeomanry. FANY was the ladies' auxiliary of the black propaganda, dirty tricks, and covert action agency Special Operations Executive, SOE. So once again, the relations between men and women become part of the story of the relations between governments.

5. ALL THE NEWS? THAT'S FIT TO PRINT

Of the five newspapers mentioned as helpmates in the secret BSC history, British Intelligence had the most ambivalent relationship with the *New York Times* and Arthur Sulzberger. A partial explanation lies in a report in the SOE archives. On September 15, 1941, SOE agent Valentine Williams wrote back to London, "I had an hour with Arthur Sulzberger, proprietor of the *New York Times*, last week. He told me that for the first time in his life he regretted being a Jew because, with the tide of anti-Semitism rising, he was unable to champion the anti-Hitler policy of the administration as vigorously and as universally as he would like as his sponsorship would be attributed to Jewish influence by isolationists and thus lose something of its force." Therefore, although British Intelligence had other contacts on the *New York Times* staff, the top man was not always on board. He sometimes got angry with his reporters, like James Reston, who cooperated with British Intelligence more closely than he liked.

6. RENDERING TO THE ROMANS

From the mid-1950s to the mid-1960s *The Rome Daily American* was a prime example of a "proprietary" Agency paper. It was finally spun off into the safe hands of an Agency friend, Samuel Meek, an executive with the advertising firm of J. Walter Thompson. JWT was very close to Western intelligence agencies. During World War II, J. Walter Thompson had been the advertising agency of choice for British Intelligence. After Mr. Meek took over official ownership, a CIA man, Robert H. Cunningham, managed the *Rome Daily American* for several years.

7. SEE THE WORLD ON 50 DOLLARS A DAY

The Fodor travel guides are so recognizable that they deserve a spot here. The CIA never actually owned these guides, but the publisher Eugene Fodor was a lieutenant in Donovan's OSS during World War II. He was very cooperative with the CIA as long as the agents' work did not interfere with their work on the guides and no politics seeped into the guides. In a 1977 *New York Times* interview, Fodor acknowledged that he allowed CIA agents to "cover" themselves in foreign countries by writing for his travel guides. They were all highly professional and did high-quality work. This reminds me of the reporter who told me that in spotting CIA people he always looked closely at the people who were overqualified or too talented for the jobs they appeared to hold. So the CIA got the cover it wanted, and Fodor got the top quality employees that made his guides sparkle. Sounds like a good marriage.

8. THE FINEST PAPER IN THE LAND—*THE NATIONAL INTELLIGENCE DAILY*

I have included this here because it is a newspaper (in a newspaper format) published daily by the CIA. The subscription list, while under 70, is the best—the president and top U.S. government officials. For timely authoritative world news, no other paper in the world matches the *National Intelligence Daily*. Wouldn't they love this baby on Wall Street?

9. HE BACKED THE BRITS

During World War II the desperate British tried to control all the American newspapers they could. The secret history of these operations recounts, "During the critical period before Pearl Harbor [hostile newspapers] represented such a grave menace that serious consideration was given to the possibility of putting them out of business. . . ." One of the publishers who was on the same wavelength with the British and "rendered service of particular value was George Backer, publisher of the *New York Post*. . . ." Like many tried and proven friends of Britain, he later became useful as propaganda policy director for the U.S. Office of War Information.

10. RALPH INGERSOLL, EDITOR OF *PM*

Ingersoll is also listed in *British Security Coordination* as having rendered the British "service of particular value." This was easy at *PM*. The owner was Marshall Field III, who had been reared in England and was close to his English cousin Ronald Tree, a major propagandist at the British Ministry of Information. Field also funded the start-up *Chicago Sun* as an interventionist rival to the isolationist *Chicago Tribune*.

Patron of Letters

Planting their views in newspapers certainly brings joy to the hearts of intelligence officers everywhere, but the real glory comes from planting books. These have a firm, lasting feel that is more likely to impress intellectuals who, being the distributors of opinion, then influence others. The CIA is said to have financed, published, or guaranteed a demand for more than a thousand books. British Intelligence probably did as well during the 20th century but their humility has kept them from claiming credit. Here are some best-sellers that few realize were plants by intelligence agencies.

1. CONNED BY TWO PSEUDO KIDS

My Sister and I: The Diary of a Dutch Boy Refugee by Dirk Van Der Heide was all the rage in early 1941. The critics fell all over themselves. "Books," in the *New York Herald Tribune,* where British Intelligence was planting items at will, said: "He has given us one of the most balanced, sensible, and enlightened reports to come out of chaos." The *Boston Transcript* wrote: "This small diary will take you about an hour to read, and about a lifetime to forget. . . ." The *Nation* wrote "A document you will never forget. . . . It is a book of both human and historical significance." *The Christian Century*: "An authentic document which brings the experience of European refugee children vividly before the mind of the American reader." There was even an immensely popular song in the summer of 1941—"My Sister and I"—whose title page reads "As inspired by the current best-seller." Those who heard this emotional tune say there was not a dry eye in the house when it was finished.

My Sister and I is the story of the escape from Holland of 12-year-old Dirk and his 9-year-old sister Ketene. The Germans are cowardly killers, the British are helpful and cheerful as the children make their way first to England and then to the United States. A great story, it whipped up a tremendous amount of anti-German and pro-English feeling, but it was completely fictitious. It is unknown how many of the reviewers were, in the intelligence phrase, "witting." The author was not a 12-year-old boy but a middle-aged editor at Harcourt Brace named Stanley Preston Young. With the encouragement of a colleague, Frank Morley, Young wrote this tearjerker for Sir William Stephenson "Intrepid," who ran British Intelligence in the United States. Stephenson was most anxious to break down American resistance to American participation in the war. Paul Fussell has a more detailed version of this story in his wonderful book, *Thank God for the Atom Bomb and other Essays*.

2. DEAR DIARY—*THE PENKOVSKY PAPERS*

Published by Doubleday in 1965, this book purports to be the diary of Colonel Oleg Penkovsky, the Soviet Intelligence officer who told all to British and American Intelligence in the early 1960s. His information is reputed to have been essential to President Kennedy during the Cuban Missile Crisis in October 1962. There was no such diary. Penkovsky was daring, but not crazy, and a spy would have to be crazy to keep so incriminating a document as a diary. What the CIA had were the transcripts of hours of debriefings of Penkovsky and copies of documents he had passed to them. The men who shaped this material into diary form were Frank Gibney, then working for *The Chicago Daily News,* and a KGB defector named Peter Deriabin. Doubleday pleads ignorance about the CIA's role here. The real intelligence cognoscenti spotted the CIA's hand early on because the book follows the CIA stylebook for changing spellings from the Cyrillic alphabet.

3.   WRITE IT AND REVIEW IT—THE FULL TREATMENT

One way to be sure the books you finance get good reviews is to write them yourself. Once again, a thorough investigation would show how British Intelligence pioneered this ploy, but the OSS/CIA people were exceptional students. One CIA-financed book was *Escape from Red China* published by Coward, McCann and Geoghegan. The author, Robert Loh, gives a very vivid description of his life in China including his experience of being brainwashed—very graphic, depressing stuff. The *New York Times* of November 11, 1962, carried a favorable review of this volume by another CIA man, Richard L. Walker.

4.   ON THE TIGER'S BACK

Another CIA volume that did well was *On the Tiger's Back,* purportedly written by one Aderogba Ajao, a Nigerian who had studied at an East German university. This experience seems to have rid him of illusions about the glories of Soviet-style socialism—just the sort of story the CIA loved to have others tell.

5. **PRAEGER AND** *THE NEW CLASS*

In an interview published on December 26, 1977, Frederick Praeger the publisher told the *New York Times* that Milovan Djillis's book *The New Class* was their first book project that the CIA had a hand in, though he professed that at the time he had "no idea there was a CIA." He added that he later published about 25 volumes in which the CIA had an interest. Djilas was a disillusioned Yugoslavian official who wrote about his personal experiences that had led him to reject Communism.

The story goes that by the time he finished the manuscript Mr. Djillis was under such a cloud that Praeger could not get the last 100 or so pages out of Yugoslavia. Praeger appealed to the U.S. government, and the missing pages were apparently carried out of Yugoslavia to Austria by *Time* correspondent Edgar Clark and his wife. Though Mr. Clark and his wife profess no knowledge, the manuscript ended up in the CIA's hands, then Praeger's hands, and then in the hands of numerous foreign publishers courtesy of CIA man Arthur Cox, who, posing as a Praeger official, sold it to numerous foreign publishers.

6. **THE BUCKLEY WAY**

Actually the book was *The Yenan Way* by Eudocio Ravines. The fact that the translation was by William F. Buckley Jr., a CIA man in the early 1950s, has only leaked out recently. Mr. Buckley is more renowned as a conservative TV commentator and the editor of *National Review*, the conservative journal his family owns. *The Yenan Way* received much praise for its clear and vivid writing. One wonders how much credit for this good writing should go to Eudocio Ravines and how much to Mr. Buckley. Ravines was a onetime top Communist organizer in Latin America who lost faith in Communism and Stalin.

7. GETTING READY FOR NAM

North Vietnam Today: Profile of a Communist State was published in 1962 by that faithful CIA publisher Frederick A. Praeger. In many ways a warm-up for Vietnam propaganda, the book was by P. J. Honey. Most of the book had originally been published in another CIA organ, the periodical *China Quarterly*.

8. THE FUTURE OF COMMUNIST SOCIETY

Another Praeger offering, *The Future of Communist Society* was published in 1961 and written by Walter Laqueur and Leopold Labedz. It was a reprint of a special issue of another CIA periodical called *Survey*.

9. THE SINO-SOVIET DISPUTE

This 1961 Praeger book was attributed to a triumvirate of authors: G.F. Hudson, Richard Lowenthal, and Roderick MacFarquhar. It had also been published as a special issue of *China Quarterly*. Few but the CIA would have had the incentive to put 200 translated pages of Chinese and Soviet documents on the record for English-speaking specialists.

10. OXFORD UNIVERSITY PRESS GETS ITS CHANCE

Praeger didn't get all the CIA publishing business. The university presses also got to belly up to the trough occasionally. The book here in question is *World Communism: The Disintegration of a Secular Faith* by Richard Lowenthal. This was imprinted as an Encounter Book. *Encounter* was a highbrow intellectual journal, the leading light in the CIA's galaxy of publications.

"The Company" and "The Friends" Take to the Air

G ood propaganda must envelop the target, must blanket the mark. Everywhere the target audience turns the propagandist's version of the story must flood every venue from which information flows. Once periodicals, newspapers, and books were covered, could radio be far behind? The British once again blazed the propaganda trail and the rich Americans made the trail into a superhighway.

1. BRITISH INTELLIGENCE OF THE AMERICAN AIRWAVES—WRUL

"By the middle of 1941," notes a recently released British document, "station WRUL was virtually . . . a subsidiary of BSC, sending out British propaganda all over the world." British Security Coordination (BSC) was the umbrella organization representing all British Intelligence organizations in the Western Hemisphere from its headquarters in Rockefeller Center in New York City. Its head was a tough Canadian businessman named William Stephenson, better known by his telex address "Intrepid." With its 50,000 watts of power, WRUL of

Boston was the most powerful shortwave station in the Americas and probably the world in 1940. It received 20,000 foreign fan letters a year. Through the cooperation of WRUL's owner Walter Lemmon, an IBM executive, BSC used this powerful propaganda tool to broadcast in 22 different languages and dialects. WRUL set the model for later CIA radio work, but Lemmon was still denying any knowledge of British Intelligence involvement when questioned in the late 1960s. BSC used WRUL to support all sorts of other propaganda operations, such as the campaign to keep Spain out of the war. The station's rule that it could broadcast no material unless that material had appeared in the American press was easily circumvented by planting articles in papers such as the *New York Herald Tribune*, the *New York Times*, the *Baltimore Sun*, or a half-dozen other BSC-friendly American papers. By late 1941, William Donovan and the American OSS were also working behind the scenes with BSC to use WRUL. Finally, it was taken over by the U.S. government after Pearl Harbor. Even as late, as the early 1960s, the CIA was still using WRUL for propaganda broadcasts against Fidel Castro.

2. SOLDIER SEND-UP FROM LONDON

Soldatensender Calais, "German Soldiers Radio Calais," was just one of an array of creative gems from the devious mind of Sefton Delmer, in normal life Berlin bureau chief for Lord Beaverbrook's *Daily Express*. The station was, of course, a hoax. It was not a soldier's radio. It was not German. It did not broadcast from Calais, but from near London. Its major voice, a purported German officer, *Der Chief*, was just as phony as the rest of it. As Delmer told one prospective recruit "I must warn you that in my unit we are up to all the dirty tricks we can devise. No holds barred. The dirtier the better. Lies, treachery, everything."

Der Chief succeeded not by speaking against Hitler but by pretending to endorse the Furhrer and his war. Der Chief lamented, "Our brave soldiers freezing to death," on the Eastern Front because traitors on the home front delayed production of winter uniforms to make more money on them. Had traitorous submarine crews delayed their going to sea by sabotaging their subs? Der Chief went into instructive detail on how the sabotage was carried out. Der Chief gave the same tongue-lashing to all sorts of profiteering and self-serving deeds that sapped the German war effort. Soldatensender Calais gave daily lessons in sabotage, malingering, and general goofing off under the guise of delivering patriotic diatribes against these very actions. This was called "operational propaganda"—propaganda that persuaded the listener to do bad things. Black propaganda at its best.

3. BROTHER OF SOLDATENSENDER— ATLANTIKSENDER

Atlantiksender had a Der Chief clone—Colonel Spraggett. But its specialty was news broadcasts to sap German morale and the war effort. Often these were contrived eyewitness reports of bombings and the like to make it sound as if the British knew everything. It also told its listeners in both medium- and shortwave that prisoners held by the British and Americans were attending the excellent trade and professional schools set up in the prison camps. In addition, many of the prisoners were earning dollars working outside the camps and would have a big advantage after the war when the mark was worthless.

4. PROPAGANDA FOR THE PIOUS—"CHRIST THE KING"

Delmer neglected no one. All who listened got an earful of irrelevant truths and plausible sounding whoppers. If *Atlantiksender* and *Soldatensender* appealed to the listeners' self-interest and greed, then "Christ the King" appealed to their "humanitarian conscience." Who would possibly be broadcasting such material during the war? Delmer had the SOE rumor mill spread the word across Europe that this was a black radio station secretly run by Vatican radio and thus evidence that the pope was against Hitler and the Nazis. The speaker was a "priest" named "Father Andreas."

5. THE CIA AND THE SOVIET STATE SEE THAT SOVIET CITIZENS GET THE NEWS

This is a tale of woe and incompetence to gladden the heart of any bureaucracy hater. During the 1940s and 1950s, one part of the Soviet state apparatus was spending millions of rubles to jam Western shortwave radio broadcasts from the BBC, Radio Free Europe, and Radio Liberty. Meanwhile another branch of the Soviet government was working diligently to provide millions of cheap shortwave radios for Soviet citizens. In 1953, three years or so after the CIA's Radio Free Europe got going, the USSR Council of Ministers caught on and told the Ministry of Communications to stop producing radios capable of receiving Western broadcasts. Not only did the Ministry of Communications forget to stop production, it actually increased production to four million radios a year. To make matters worse, the Soviet government belatedly discovered that almost 90 percent of these radios were in the western part of the USSR where the Soviet's own broadcast could not be heard, only stations like Radio Free Europe and Radio Liberty. Ahh—the joys of a command economy.

6. THE COMPANY BEGETS RADIO FREE EUROPE

In 1950 the CIA set up a front, the "National Committee for a Free Europe," to own and operate Radio Free Europe (RFE). President of the committee was the old World War II propaganda hand C. D. Jackson of Time-Life, Inc. He brought General Eisenhower onto the board of directors of the "National Committee for a Free Europe (when he became president in 1953, Eisenhower made Jackson Special Advisor to the President for Psychological Warfare).

With a generous budget of roughly $70 million in 2003 dollars, Radio Free Europe soon had 29 stations broadcasting with all the sophistication and slickness of American advertising in 16 languages. RFE was a major force creating discontent in Eastern Europe, even encouraging revolution. Some who participated in the 1956 Hungarian Revolution remember RFE encouraging revolution and even promising armed support. The CIA denies this but control of RFE was lax at best. Strangely, the transcripts are missing for those days in October–November. The CIA ran RFE through the 1970s when it was turned over to the private financing it was always supposed to have had.

7. RADIO LIBERTY TAKES ON THE BIG KAHOONA

Where Radio Free Europe was directly targeted at the Soviet satellite nations, Radio Liberty went directly after the Soviet Union. Radio Liberty was only one of a stable of anti-Soviet outfits dependent on the generosity of the "American Committee for Liberation (ACL)." Another project that sprang from the ACL was "The Institute for the Study of the USSR," which from its base in Munich distributed the well-respected reference source, *Who's Who in the USSR.*

8. RADIO SWAN SINGS TO FIDEL

In the run-up to the 1961 Bay of Pigs invasion the CIA used a bevy of stations—WMIE and WGBS in Miami, WKWF in Key West, WWL in New Orleans, WRUL in New York, and Radio SWAN on a Caribbean island—to broadcast propaganda at Cuba and anyone else in Latin America who would listen. A steamship company in New York ostensibly owned radio SWAN, but the company had not owned any steamships in years. Another problem was the wonderful clarity of SWAN's signal, which attracted a flock of advertisers begging to have their commercial messages sent to all of Latin America. The CIA eventually had to accept advertising, fearing that to refuse would endanger Radio SWAN's already thin cover.

9. RADIO FREE ASIA—AND THAT WAS THE PROBLEM

Radio Free Asia (RFA) began in 1951 with the goal of being the Asian equivalent of Radio Free Europe or Radio Liberty. RFA had a wonderful transmitter in Manila. Its CIA funding came through the typical front—the "Committee for Free Asia." Everything looked great. There was one problem, however, that no one noticed until the project was well along—China was a radio-free zone. The poverty-stricken people of China had very few radios. In addition, the Chinese Communist authorities were not about to fix this situation. Where are the Soviets when you need them?

The CIA solution was to float radios into China on balloons from the offshore island of Formosa. However, the wind, which moved from west to east, blew the radios back out to Formosa rather than into China as planned. With no audience, the station wandered along until the mid-1950s when the CIA pulled the plug. The "Committee for a Free Asia," changed its name to the Asia Foundation, which was then headed for years by an "ex-CIA," man Robert Blum. Eventually the foundation broke its ties to the CIA.

10. WE DO IT IN FARSI, TOO—RADIO LIBERATION

Radio Liberation was a CIA operation to broadcast anti-Khomeini broadcasts from Egypt into Iran.

From "A Better World," "A World Full of Bliss" to a "Wet Job" and "The Measles"

All of these terms are spookspeak for assassination. The Eastern Europeans, the French, and to a lesser extent the British have used killing as a handy way to eliminate problems. When the CIA was trying to build more capability in this area in the late 1950s the Company's James Angleton and William Harvey consulted British Intelligence officer Peter Wright (later author of *Spycatcher*). "The French," replied Wright, "have you tried them? Its more their type of thing, you know. . . . We are out of that game. We're the junior partner in the alliance, remember? It's your responsibility now."

Determining when assassination has taken place is more difficult than it might at first appear given the KGB tactics and its motto: "Any fool can commit a murder; it takes an artist to commit a suicide." In writing about this tool of foreign policy one is always confronted by the idealistic assertion voiced by British Prime Minister Benjamin Disraeli: "Assassination never changed the history of the world." The sad fact is that assassinations have changed the world. When confronted with the fact that certain assassinations did change the course of history—the assassination of Archduke Franz Ferdinand and his wife in June 1914 that brought on World War I is an example—skeptics usually assert that the war would have happened anyway. This assertion is, of course, impossible to prove or disprove. It is the sort of statement you can get away with in academia if you assert that you are taking a moral stance against such dirty work as assassination. Have no doubt—this is dirty work.

1. WE DIDN'T PULL THE TRIGGER—INTREPID DID IT FOR US

During World War II, and particularly before the United States officially declared war in December of 1941, British Intelligence, namely British Security Coordination, ran a very powerful operation in the United States with the go-ahead from President Franklin Roosevelt. The head of BSC, William Stephenson (Intrepid) ran a hard-nosed operation in his efforts to protect British interests and bring the United States into the war. As he relates in his book *Spycatcher*, Peter Wright mentioned this to the CIA's William Harvey and James Angleton when they sought help with assassinations: "Have you thought of approaching Stephenson?" I asked. "A lot of the old-timers say he ran this kind of thing in New York during the war. . . ."

2. DEFENESTRATION

This wonderful word, that one might appropriately find on a college board exam, means the act of throwing a person out a window. The act has a long if not honored history. In fact, it is almost a Prague tradition. The "defenestration of Prague," the throwing out the window of three of archduke Ferdinand's regents in 1618 started the very bloody Thirty Years' War. The war left the central European countryside devastated and nearly a third of the German population dead. Three hundred years later, in 1948, the fatal defenestration of Jan Masaryk, the nonCommunist foreign minister, took place 12 days after the Communists had taken over Czechoslovakia. He was the optimistic, witty son of the first Czech president, Tomas Masaryk and the active lover of the American writer Marsha Davenport. The state police quickly closed the case. It does take an artist to commit a suicide.

3. DEFENESTRATION—A RECENT LEAP

In 1983 London's Midland Bank received word that its resident manager in Moscow, Dennis Skinner, had fallen to his death from his upper floor flat. The Soviets said no crime had been committed, but a London coroner's jury brought back a verdict of "unlawful death." Some experts class this as the classic artistic KGB suicide and a return to the tried and true post–World War II defenestration. Banks like Midland have long supplied cover for British and American Intelligence, so the thought is that Skinner was such a person. He was also dangerous to the Soviets. Two days before his leap he had warned London that there was a Soviet spy in the British Embassy. He went off the building before revealing the name, or so the story goes.

4. DAMOCLES

Damocles, if you remember your Greek literature, was seated at a banquet with a sword suspended over his head by a single hair. This was to emphasize to him the perilous nature of life. In the early 1960s, Damocles was the name of an assassination campaign run by Israeli Intelligence against German rocket scientists working for the Arabs. The fear was that the German scientists would build a V-2 rocket that would hang over the head of Israel. The letter bomb was the weapon of choice. After the death of several Egyptian officers and the wounding of several German scientists the Germans were sufficiently intimidated, and the program failed.

5. A NICE SIMPLE MOTIVE—MONEY

The spies in the British government in the 1930s, '40s, and '50s worked for the Soviets largely for ideological reasons. Communism and sympathy for that vanguard of the proletariat, the Soviet Union, was very "in" with the intelligentsia of Cambridge and Oxford. Ernest Holliway Oldham was not so sensitive and caring as those from Oxbridge. After two decades as a cipher clerk in the Foreign Office in London, he was poor and determined to do something about it. On a trip to Paris, he went into the Soviet Embassy and boldly announced he had a cipher to sell. The Soviet Intelligence man in charge, Vladimir Voynovich, examined the documents, pronounced them worthless, and after copying them threw Oldham and his papers out. He did send the copies on to Moscow, which was stunned. It turned out that the cipher was priceless and Oldham was gone without a trace. A brief aside: One of the great differences between the Western and the Soviet systems is that in the West it is no crime to be an ignorant dope. Voynovich was eventually executed. The Soviets finally tracked Oldham down, stuck 2000 pounds in his hand (more than $100,000 in 2003 dollars), and he was theirs until he resigned from the Foreign Office, apparently as a way to stop working for Soviet Intelligence. He was found dead in his kitchen with his head in the oven, an apparent suicide. This head-in-the-oven trick is an old favorite with Soviet assassins. Later Oldham's wife died from a mysterious illness just before she was to identify her husband's contact for MI-5.

6. OH, THOSE SUICIDES

Samuel Ginsberg was born to a Polish Jewish family. In 1917, he joined the Bolsheviks and like many—Bronstein (Trotsky), Dzugashvili (Stalin), and Ulyanov (Lenin)—took on a *nom de revolution*, Walter Krivitsky. By the 1930s he was faithfully doing what Stalin wished as resident spymaster of the Netherlands. By 1937, he was doing such work for all of Western Europe. He remained faithful even when his friend Ignace Reiss, resident director of French networks, defected. A SMERSH assassination squad (there were three after him) soon caught up with Reiss and his body was found in Switzerland heavily weighted with submachine gun bullets.

At this point Krivitsky was summoned to return to Moscow. He had the good sense to see that this probably meant reporting for his own execution so he, too, defected. He asked for asylum in France and told interesting stories to the police. (One of these stories led police to John King, who had succeeded Oldham the Cipher Clerk in the preceding story.) Stalin took offense. Krivitsky moved and kept moving and so did the people from SMERSH. Eventually he died in a Washington, D.C., hotel where, the legal documents say, he "committed suicide."

7. THE SUPER GUNNER IS GUNNED DOWN

Dr. Gerald Bull (1928–1990) was a man with an obsession and the knowledge to build the world's largest gun, a gun so large and powerful that it could be used to launch satellites. He had been used and abused by various Western intelligence agencies including the CIA—he had even done prison time when prosecuted by the Carter administration. He ended by working for Iraq and got himself assassinated for his trouble. Bull was also a man with so much more knowledge about his subject than anyone else that his death marked the end of Iraq's attempt to build the supergun. So his work on artillery, which experts say had affected the course of two wars, was not allowed to further affect relations between Iraq and Israel.

8. BOHDAN BOLTS

On August 12, 1961, the day before the Berlin Wall went up, Bohdan Stashinsky crossed over to West Berlin. In an extraordinary confession, he told how he had assassinated two Ukrainian dissident exiles, Lev Rebet in Munich in 1957 and Stefan Bandera in 1959. His tool had been a seven-inch gun (it looks like a pipe with a lever on the side), which fired a charge, which vaporized cyanide into the victim's face. The assassin, Stashinsky, had the gun hidden in a rolled-up newspaper and caught the victims alone momentarily. The coroner declared Mr. Rebet's death a heart attack, but correctly identified Bandera's cause of death. For coming clean with the details, Mr. Stashinsky received a short prison sentence.

9. DEATH BY BUMBERSHOOT

Georgi Markov was a Bulgarian dissident leader, an author and playwright, living in London. One day as he stood by the Waterloo Bridge a man poked him in the leg with an umbrella, apologized, and went on his way. Mr. Markov soon died. His death was baffling, so he was buried. Later the body was exhumed and a small hollow pellet was found in his leg. The pellet had been filled with a deadly poison called ricin, a protein extracted from the bean of the castor oil plant. The KGB had supplied the umbrella to the Bulgarians from its supply of such innovative and groundbreaking toys.

10. NICE TRIES—ATTEMPT NUMBER 32

According to one source, there were 31 attempts on the life of French President Charles de Gaulle. De Gaulle was usually regarded as pro-Palestinian, but during the Arab-Israeli Six-Day War of June 1967, he retreated to enigmatic neutrality, which irritated the defeated Arabs and their Soviet Allies and surrogates. The Czechs set out to blow up the Grand Charles as he placed a wreath on a French war memorial near Beirut, Lebanon. The Czechs would make this media event death serve double duty by foisting the blame onto the Mossad (Israeli Intelligence) and the CIA. The anticipated result would be a wave of anti-American and anti-Israeli demonstrations in Western Europe and the isolation of Israel. To the consternation of the Czechs, de Gaulle called a referendum just before his departure. When he did not get the backing he wanted the prickly general resigned from office, thus thwarting the plot.

They Shoot Spies, Don't They?

From time immemorial, they did—shoot them, hang them, and imaginatively torture them to death. If you were caught, death was almost routine, certainly in the Eastern bloc, until the "Espionage Revolution" of the early 1960s. With the Cold War in full swing, each side had hundreds, even thousands of agents and collaborators in the field. It finally occurred to a few brave souls that captured spies might be more useful as trade bait than as corpses.

1. "WE'VE TRADED A MASTER SPY FOR AN AIRPLANE DRIVER"

Thus exclaimed former Secretary of State Dean Acheson about the first trade of the "Espionage Revolution," that of Colonel Rudolf Abel for U-2 pilot Francis Gary Powers. Abel had been running a spy ring in New York for a number of years when finally tripped up by a defector. Powers had been overflying the Soviet Union in the high-flying U-2 when he was shot down. Even worse, Powers was captured alive and tried in court by the Soviets. Colonel Rudolf Abel (real name William Fischer) had been defended by lawyer James Donovan, a former OSS man from World War II. Unfortunately for Donovan there was just too much good evidence against Abel. Even the best lawyer could not make such a mountain of evidence go away, but Donovan did convince the judge to spare Abel's life with the plea that he might be tradable for an American spy at some time in the future. That future came in 1962 when Donovan and East German lawyer Wolfgang Vogel cut a deal to exchange Powers for Abel. The prisoner exchange on the Glienicke Bridge, soon called the "Bridge of Spies," that connected the divided city of Berlin, kicked off the Intelligence Revolution. Spies and the information they possessed had become too valuable to execute.

2. THE SWINGING SPIES ON THE GLIENICKE BRIDGE—THE LAST ACT

The last exchange on the Glienicke Bridge, an eight-spy swap, was on February 11, 1986. Going east, in the featured exchange, were Czech Intelligence agents Karl F. Koecher (age 52) and his sexy wife Hana (age 40) with her "incredibly large blue eyes." Going west was the famous Soviet dissident Nathan Sharansky. Little was then known publicly of Koecher and his wife, only that he was a Czech Intelligence agent who had worked for the CIA in the 1970s. Later it came out that he was the only known Eastern Bloc agent to penetrate the CIA. And a brilliant penetration it was—20 years as an illegal operating in New York and Washington with hardly a misstep.

The Koechers' saga had started with their phony 1965 defection from Czechoslovakia. They entered the United States in December of 1965. Apparently, the first idea was to build Koecher up as an academic. This

Central Intelligence Agency

Francis Gary Powers beside his U-2 spy plane. When this photo was taken, the U-2 project was one of the most secret operations in the world. Powers was shot down by the Soviets in May 1960. This incident caused President Eisenhower's Paris summit with Soviet premier Nikita Khrushchev to dissolve in an uproar.

went well at first. There was a stint at Indiana University, then a Ph.D. from Columbia where he was a student of Zbigniew Brzezinski, later President Jimmy Carter's National Security Advisor. Here Koecher ran into an unforeseen impediment to his academic aspirations. He posed as an outspoken anti-Communist, apparently not realizing that such a philosophical stand was sure death to tenure hopes or even long-term employment at most American universities. The chairman of the humanities department at the Old Westbury campus of the State University of New York even told a *New York Times* reporter that "Mr. Koecher's anti-Communist positions" were one reason they let him go.

In 1973, the Koechers moved to Washington, D.C., where the CIA hired him as a contract translator and then transferred him back to New York as an analyst. He and his beautiful wife were never low key in the classic deep cover spy model. They were swingers. They later told author Ronald Kessler that at least once or twice a week they had other couples over for dinner and spouse-swapping sex. This along with larger sex parties and orgies went on in both New York and Washington. Karl and Hana also admit they saw a lot of the New York sex clubs Plato's Retreat and Hellfire. Washingtonians will be gratified to know that such experienced European bed hoppers declare Washington the "sex capital of the world."

Mr. Koecher admits that he did take time from this demanding sex schedule to do "incalculable damage to the CIA and its assets." For example, some of his translating work was on documents from the CIA's major asset in Moscow, Aleksandr Ogorodnik. Koecher told the Soviets who caught Mr. Ogorodnik. Seeing that the jig was up Ogorodnik took a pill from a pen that the CIA had given him, and in 10 seconds he was dead. How did a career so full of personal and professional gratification end? Apparently the FBI caught on when it identified Karl as the man who was having "brush encounters" with Czech Intelligence officers. Once onto Karl, FBI surveillance revealed Hana also making "brush encounters" and filling dead drops. In 1984 the FBI picked the couple up and questioned them thoroughly. It seems they disregarded all FBI and Justice Department guidelines on such interviews. At any rate, a deal was finally cut and one fine November morning the Koechers took their final Mercedes ride from West to East on the Glienicke Bridge.

3. GORDON LONSDALE BY ANY OTHER NAME

Gordon Lonsdale aka Konon Molody was a KGB spymaster in Great Britain. From 1955 to 1961, he ran a ring of spies gathering information on British under-water submarine detection device research at the Admiralty Underwater Weapons Establishment at Port-land. He was captured in 1961 and given a long prison sentence but exchanged for Englishman Grenville Wynne in 1964. Wynne was a very visible businessman who drove a sort of trade fair on wheels, showing British export products throughout Eastern Europe. The truck, the longest of its type ever produced in England, had been paid for in full by MI-6. As such, he was part of one of the most productive operations ever run by the West behind the Iron Curtain. Wynne was caught by the KGB as the contact for Oleg Penkovsky, the Soviet Intelligence officer who had told the West of the number and size of Soviet missiles. This was the vital informa-tion that allowed U.S. President John Kennedy to call Khrushchev's bluff in the Cuban Missile Crisis of 1962. Penkovsky did not do as well as Wynne, but Wynne had no picnic after his capture. Penkovsky was reportedly thrown alive into a crematory furnace. Wynne was shattered by the effects of his incarceration and interro-gation at the KGB's Lubyanka headquarters.

4. A CORPSE FOR TWO

One need not be alive to be traded for failed agents who are (alive). The deceased, ostensibly one Ute Schwartz, was killed by a taxi in West Berlin in 1968. Ute's relatives, when informed, replied that she was very much alive. Upon closer examination the dead Ute's passport and other documents proved to be

phony; there were ciphers and East German addresses
cleverly hidden in her effects. After considerable
sleuthing, the body was identified as that of an East
German illegal (an agent who operates outside the embassy and without diplomatic immunity) named Gu
drun Heidle. Dr. Wolfgang Vogel again presided over
the exchange—certainly a strange one. The deceased
was exchanged for two West Germans arrested by the
East Germans.

5. An EVEN TRADE—MASTER SPIES FOR A MAILMAN

We have met these two beauties before. At various
times they went by the names Lona and Morris, Helen
and Peter, Volunteer and Lesley, and Israel and Shirley.
By any name, they were veteran Soviet agents in
America and England, Morris and Lona Cohen. Morris
was a veteran of the Spanish Civil War. Both he and
Lona had worked to steal atomic secrets during the
1940s and both skedaddled from New York in 1950 as
the Feds closed in on their cohorts the Rosenbergs and
other atom spies.

They resurfaced in 1954 as the Krogers in England
and after a good run to 1961, they were captured as
part of the Portland spy ring that had busied itself stealing secrets from the Admiralty's Underwater Weapons
Establishment at Portland. Their fingerprints allowed
FBI/MI-5 to unravel their identities and travels and got
them 20 years hard time. After only eight years, they
walked in exchange for a hapless British college professor, Gerald Brooke, who had been caught in the
USSR mailing anti-Soviet pamphlets. The Soviets re-
galed these talented veteran spies with great honors:
the Order of the Red Banner, given for bravery in com-

bat or behind enemy lines; and the highest medal for bravery, The Gold Star Hero of the Russian Federation—all certainly well merited. There is no record of what medals Professor Brooke merited or received.

6. ZAKHAROV FOR DANILOFF THE PAWN

One disquieting aspect of these trades is that the West seems rarely to have gotten good value for the well-trained Eastern Bloc agents we sent home. Dean Acheson's characterization of the Rudolf Abel for Gary Powers trade as that of a master spy for an airplane driver may have been harsh, but there was some truth to it. We often seemed to receive Soviet malcontents or some innocent pawn swept up by the KGB for trade bait. For instance, the FBI arrested Gennadi Zakharov who had been passed phony documents on the F-15 fighter by an FBI counterspy, one Leakh N. Bhoge. The Soviets were good at the drill by 1986. They immediately swept up Nicolas Daniloff, *U.S. News and World Report*'s man in Moscow. They took him right off a Moscow street, put him in handcuffs, and held him on spy charges in prison. A month later, on September 29, 1986, the deal was done and Daniloff was on his way out of the USSR.

7. THE PROFESSOR GETS A GIFT

In 1963 the FBI arrested Igor Ivanov, who appeared to be a lowly chauffeur for Armtog, the Soviet trading company. He was really a Soviet spy, the real item. They had him, and he had no diplomatic immunity. Shortly thereafter, a Yale professor visiting the Soviet Union, Frederic Barghoorn, was minding his own business when a Soviet citizen thrust a bunch of papers into his hands. These, of course, were state secrets and the

KGB representatives who happened to be handy arrested the good professor. President Kennedy made a personal appeal for Professor Barghoorn and he was soon released. Being a more legalistic people we observed the formalities of a trial for Ivanov, but after the conviction he was released to the Soviet Embassy and went home.

8. HARVESTING THE HARVESTER MAN

In May of 1978 a Soviet diplomat, Vladimir Zinyakin, and two Soviet international employees of the United Nations, Rudolf Chernyayev and Valdik Enger, were arrested at a Woodbridge, New Jersey, shopping center while passing $16,000 to retired Navy Lieutenant Commander Arthur Lindberg for submarine secrets. Unknown to the Soviets, the commander was whiling away his retirement working for the FBI. Unlike Zinyakin, who had diplomatic immunity, Enger and Chernyayev were open to prosecution. Back in Moscow, the KGB dragged International Harvester man F. J. Crawford from a car and charged him with smuggling, later changed to currency violations—apparently because it would be simpler to fabricate a case.

As evidence of his faith in the efficiency of the Soviet justice system Soviet President Leonid Brezhnev pronounced Crawford guilty before the "trial." Brezhnev proved prophetic. The two Soviets got a tough-sounding 50 years from an American court. But it did not matter—all were released to the custody of their embassies. The Democratic Carter administration wanted more than a businessman in the deal. Thus the Soviets sent the United States an eclectic collection of five dissidents—a Baptist, up for missionary activity; a human rights activist; a pilot who had plotted to defect by hijacking a plane; a Ukrainian propagandist; and another hijack plotter. The final exchange was consummated in an airplane hangar at New York's Kennedy International Airport.

9. MEGASWAP, JUNIOR

The last swap between East and West Germany, just before Christmas 1989, was a large last gasp. The Communists made up for the poor quality of their goods by sheer volume. The total deal was four in exchange for 125. The direct swap was four agents held by the West in exchange for 25 "agents" held by the Communists. As additional bait, the Communists threw in 100 political prisoners with, I am sure, a sigh of good riddance.

10. VOGEL THE SWAPPER MAKES HIS BIGGEST DEAL

Who could forget our East German Communist friend, lawyer Wolfgang Vogel, who helped to kick off the spy swap of Rudolf Abel for Gary Powers? Vogel became a rich capitalist by arranging these deals. The least known was the biggest—250,000 East German dissidents, clergymen, and assorted know-it-alls for three billion Marks. Though it has the sound of a slave auction in the Old South, we should delicately mention price. Medical doctors, depending on specialty and condition, brought 100,000 Marks, with lower prices for those who plied less prestigious trades. In some cases, deals were made for goods that were in short supply or did not work in East Germany—coffee, bananas, elevators.

Great Quips from the Great Game

The espionage game has occupied the thoughts of some of history's great minds. Here are some of the things they have said.

1. Oh what a tangled web we weave
   When first we practice to deceive;
   But when you've practiced quite a bit
   You really get quite good at it.—*Nicholas Elliott*

2. "The trade of spy is very fine. . . . Is it not, in fact, enjoying the excitement of a thief, while still retaining the character of an honest citizen? . . . the only excitement which can compare with it is that of the life of a gambler."—*Honore de Balzac*

3. "The game of Espionage is too dirty for anyone but a gentleman."—*Anonymous British Intelligence Officer*

4. "If I lead, follow me. If I stumble, help me. If I fall behind kill me."—Counterinsurgency motto in *A Guatemala Officer and the CIA* by Tim Weiner

5. "Both virgins and fortresses are lost as soon as negotiations begin."—Benjamin Franklin

6. "Secrecy is as essential to Intelligence as vestments and incense to a mass, or darkness to a spiritual séance, and must at all costs be maintained, quite irrespective of whether or not it serves any purpose."—Malcolm Muggeridge, *The Infernal Grove*

7. "If there were no knaves, honest men should hardly come by the truth of any enterprise against them."—Sir Francis Walsingham, Spymaster for England's Queen Elizabeth I

8. "There are five kinds of spy: local spies, inside spies, reverse spies, dead spies and living spies. When the five kinds of spies are all active, no one knows their routes—this is the very essence of organizational genius, and gives leaders a major advantage. Local spies are hired from among the people of a locality. Inside spies are hired from among enemy officials. Dead spies transmit false intelligence to enemy spies. Living spies come back to report."—Sunzu

9. "The necessity of procuring good intelligence is apparent and need not be further urged. . . . Upon secrecy success depends in most enterprises. . . . And for want of it, they are generally defeated, however well planned and promising a favorable issue.—George

Washington, during the American Revolution, 1775–1783.

10. "As long as there is espionage, there will be Romeos seducing unsuspecting Juliets with access to secrets. After all I was running an intelligence service, not a lonely hearts club."—Markus Wolf, head of the East German's Foreign Intelligence Service, in his book, *Man Without a Face*

Creativity at the Bureau

During my college days the anti-Vietnam war, anti-government movement was very big in intellectual circles. The intelligence community came in for a good share of bashing. The FBI took much of the brunt of this. Not only were its operations said to be immoral and illegal, but its agents were staid, unimaginative gumshoes, who dressed wrong, had short hair, had gone to the wrong schools, and thus had not had a new idea in decades. The antiwar people set out to prove this by publishing FBI documents gained through Freedom of Information Act requests or congressional investigations. The following letters do have an immoral, "dirty tricks" feel to them, but they certainly dispel the notion that FBI men and women lacked creativity or imagination. These are taken from *Book III, Final Report of the Select Committee to Study Governmental Operations with Respect to Intelligence Activities, United States Senate, 94th Congress 2nd Session, Senate Report No. 94-755.*

1. LETTER FROM A SOUL SISTER

The following letter was sent by the FBI to the husband of a white woman activist who was apparently a very

189

effective organizer and corresponding secretary for ACTION, a black new left group. She was also active in antiwar, antidraft groups. Hubby was apparently already uneasy about her activities when he received this little missive:

> Dear Mr. . . . . . .
>
> Look man I guess your old lady doesn't get enough at home or she wouldn't be shucking and jiving with our Black men in ACTION, you dig? Like all she wants to integrate is the bedroom and us Black Sisters aint gonna take second best from our men. So lay it on her, man—or get her the hell off Newstead.
>
> A Soul Sister

The husband did not take this note very well and soon the couple was separated.

2. EQUAL OPPORTUNITY LITERARY WORK

The left was active and visible in the 1960s, so much of the FBI's efforts were directed at them. The FBI did not discriminate, though, it also exercised its creative writing skills on the right wing as seen in this 1966 letter to the wife of the Grand Dragon of the United Klans of America.

> Dear Mrs . . . .
>
> I write this letter to you only after a long period of praying to God. I must clense [sic] my soul of these thoughts. I certainly do not want to create problems inside a family but I owe a duty to the klans and its principles as well as to my own menfolk who have cast their devine [sic] lot with the klans.
>
> Your husband came to [deleted] about a year

ago and my menfolk blindly followed his leadership, believing him to be the savior of this country. They never believed the stories that he stole money from the klans in [deleted] or that he is now making over $25,000 a year. They never believed the stories that your house in [deleted] has a new refrigerator, washer, dryer, and yet one year ago, was threadbare. They refused to believe that your husband now owns three cars and a truck, including the new white car. But I believe all these things and can forgive them for a man wants to do for his family in the best way he can.

I don't have any of these things and I don't grudge you any of them neither. But your husband has been committing the greatest of the sins of our Lord for many years. He has taken the flesh of another unto himself.

Yes, Mrs . . . . he has been committing adultery. My menfolk say they don't believe this but I think they do. I feel like crying. I saw her with my own eyes. They call her Ruby. Her last name is something like [deleted] Street in [deleted] I know this. I saw her strut around at a rally with her lustful eyes and smart aleck figure.

I cannot stand for this. I will not let my husband and two brothers stand side by side with your husband and this woman in the gloris [sic] robes of the klan. . . .

I am a loyal klanswoman and a good churchgoer. I feel this problem affects the future of our great country. I hope I do not cause you harm by this and if you believe in the Good Book as I do, you may soon receive your husband back into the fold. I pray for you and your beautiful little children and

only wish I could tell you who I am. I will soon, but I
am afraid my own men would be harmed If I do.

A God-fearing klanswoman

3. FROM A CONCERNED FRIEND TO THE BILLPAYERS BACK HOME

This 1968 note (from the FBI) to the parents of an antiwar protester at Oberlin College in Ohio is certainly a
classic of the genre. In contrast with the Klan letter
above, this note is more literate and catches the tone
of Oberlin. (I was very briefly a student at Oberlin.) Not
only is Oberlin a literate place, but political and social
activism have a long and honored place in the school's
history.

Oberlin, Ohio

Dear Mr. And Mrs. Kaza:

I have thought a lot about writing to you concerning John and I have hesitated fearing my motives may be misconstrued. His present actions,
however, and the danger they offer both to his
health and personal future now prompt me to write
in the belief that you may not be aware of John's
current involvement in left-wing activities.

John and several other Oberlin students have
begun a hungerstrike to demonstrate their feelings
about the war in Vietnam. I too oppose this war but
I believe opposition should be expressed in more
responsible ways. I am also concerned about John
since the fasting he is undergoing is obviously af-
fecting his health. There is also the question of mo-
tivation for this demonstration which, it is widely
rumored on campus, is guided and directed by a

left-wing group called the Young Socialist Alliance. In his idealism I am afraid John is unwittingly becoming involved in a group that is merely using him for its own selfish purposes.

I hope you will understand my motives in writing this letter anonymously since I have John's friendship and, under the conditions of his present attitude, I doubt that he would be sympathetic to my revealing his activities to his parents. I thought, however, that you should know.

Sincerely,
A concerned friend

4. HELPING WIVES UNDERSTAND THEIR HUSBANDS' WORK

Not only white husbands, but black wives received thoughtful, FBI-prepared notes to better help them understand their spouses' time away from home. This was written to the wife of a black activist in one of the multitude of organizations that sprang up during the Vietnam War. The organization was called "Black Liberators." The wife in this case was apparently churchgoing and respectable.

Sister

Us Black Liberators are trained to respect Black Women and special are wifes and girls. Brother . . . . keeps tellin the Brothers this but he dont treet you that way. I only been in the organization 2 months but . . . . . . been maken it here with Sister Marva Bas + Sister tony and than he gives us this jive bout their better in bed than you an how he keeps you off his back by senden you a little dough ever now an then—

He says he gotta send you money [or] the Draft boards gonna chuck him in the army [or] somethen. This aint rite and were sayen that . . . is treeten you wrong—

A Black Liberator

5. TO A BLACK PANTHER WITH THOUGHTFULNESS

This letter was only part of the effort against the Black Panther Party. The letter, to a New Jersey Black Panther leader, purported to be from a member of the Students for a Democratic Society (SDS), another radical student group that flourished in the late 1960s in the turmoil over the Vietnam War.

To a Former Comrade [name]

As one of "those little bourgeoisie, snooty nose"—"little schoolboys"—"little sissies" Dave Hilliard spoke of in the "Guardian" of 8/16/69, I would like to say that you and the rest of you black racist can go to hell. I stood shoulder to shoulder with Carl Nichols last year in Military Park in Newark and got my a—whipped by a Newark pig all for the cause of the wine heads like you and the rest of the black pussycats that call themselves panthers. Big dial; you have to have a three hour educational session just to teach those . . . (you all know what that means don't you! It's the first word your handkerchief head mamma teaches you) how to spell it.

Who the hell set you and the Panthers up as the vanguard of the revolutionary and disciplinary group. You can tell all those wineheads you associate with that you'll kick no one's . . . a—,' because you'd have to take a three year course in spelling to know what an a—is and three more years to be taught where it is located.

Julius Lester called the BPP the vanguard (that's leader) organization so international whore Cleaver calls him racist, now when full allegiance is not given to the Panthers, again racist. What the hell do you want? Are you getting this? Are you lost? If you're not digging then you're really hopeless.

Oh yes! We are not concerned about Hilliard's threats. Brains will win over brawn. This way the Panthers have retaliated against US is another indication. The score: US-6: Panthers-0.

Why, I read an article in the Panther paper where a California Panther sat in his car and watched his friend get shot by Karenga's group and what did he do? He run back and write a full page story about how toug the Panthers are and what they're going to do. Ha Ha—B—S—.

goodbye [name] baby—and watch out. Karenga's coming.

"Right On" as they say.

6. TO A BLACKSTONE RANGER

The report of the Senate investigation where these letters are found identifies the Blackstone Rangers as: "a Chicago gang to whom violent type activity, shooting and the like, are second nature." The basic principle of divide and conquer is certainly as old as the Roman Empire. Here the FBI is trying to set one violent group against another. Do I hear a little reprisal music?

Editor:

What's this bull—SDS outfit? I'll tell you what they has finally showed there true color White. They are just like the commies and the other white radical groups that suck up to the blacks and use us.

We voted at our meeting in Oakland for community
control over the pigs but SDS says no. Well we can
do with out them mothers. We can do it by ourselfs
OFF THE PIGS POWER TO THE PEOPLE
                                      Soul Brother Jake

7. FRUITS OF THE FORBIDDEN VINE

The FBI, of course, had the Black Panther Party under
close electronic surveillance. From this the Bureau
learned the whereabouts of a fugitive who was then arrested. Just to keep the pot boiling and spread distrust
they sent the following note to the jailed man's half
brother.

Brother:
    Jimmie was sold out by Sister [name—the
Black Panther Party leader who made the phone
call picked up by the tap] for some pig money to
pay her rent. When she don't get it that way she
takes Panther money. How come her kid sells the
paper in his school an no one bothers him. How
comes Tyler got busted up by the pigs and her kid
didn't. How comes the FBI pig fascists knew where
to bust Lonnie and Minnie way out where they were.
                                      Think baby

8. LET ME HELP YOU INTO THIS SNITCH JACKET. WE'VE TAILORED IT JUST FOR YOU

One of the worst charges against a Black Panther was
that he or she was a police informant, a "snitch." To
saddle a party member with a "snitch jacket" would
certainly reduce the person's effectiveness and might
prove fatal. This letter alleges that a Washington, D.C.,
Black Panther leader is a snitch.

Brother:

I recently read in the Black Panther newspaper about that low dog Gaines down in Texas who betrayed his people to the pigs and it reminded me of a recent incident that I should tell you about. Around the first part of Feb. I was locked up at the local pigpen when the pigs brought in this dude who told me he was a Panther. This dude who said his name was [deleted] said he was vamped on by six pigs and was brutalized by them. This dude talked real bad and said he had killed pigs and was going to get more when he got out, so I thought he probably was one of you. The morning after [name] was brought in a couple of other dudes in suits came to see him and called him out of the cell and he was gone a couple of hours. Later on these dudes came back again to see him. [Name] told me the dudes were his lawyers but they smelled like pig to me. It seems to me that you might want to look into this because I know you don't know me and I'm not a Panther but I wan to help with the cause when I can.

A lumpen brother

9. TWO DUCKS

The FBI's COINTELPRO offensive was hardly a model of tastefulness. This and the following cartoons are to be found in "Church Committee's Final Report (Senate Report No. 94-755) The "New Mobe" was the "New Mobilization Committee to End the War in Vietnam." The SWP was the "Socialist Workers Party," a Trotskyite group. The suggestion seems to be that the Socialist Workers Party is taking foul advantage of the antiwar group.

10. COINTELPRO AND THE STUDENTS FOR A DEMOCRATIC SOCIETY

This cartoon was featured on another of the FBI's flyers helping college students gain a greater understanding of SDS.

The Magnificent Five, Plus Five

The British government and British Intelligence were certainly thoroughly penetrated by the Soviet Intelligence agencies starting in the 1930s. The names of the Magnificent Five are so well known that even many college historians have heard of them (espionage and intelligence are known among specialists as the "missing dimension" of history books). The Five are Kim Philby, Guy Burgess, Donald Maclean, Anthony Blunt, and John Cairncross. For a while there was a lively cottage industry devoted to writing and speculating about these gentlemen. If a reading of John Cairncross's heavily censored FBI file is any indication we still do not publicly know much of what he was doing even half a dozen years after his death.

Those recruited at Britain's exclusive Cambridge and Oxford Universities during the 1930s were ideological recruits attracted to Communism as the answer to the world's woes as they saw them during the Great Depression. Others of note were George Blake, atom scientist Klaus Fuchs, and the Naval Intelligence clerk Christopher John Vassall. The British Intelligence agencies were particularly vulnerable because of their recruiting practices—the right people from the right schools with the right social connections. This applied to both men and women, although MI-5 women also needed to have good legs.

1. HAROLD ADRIAN RUSSELL PHILBY (1912–1988)

Called "Kim," after Rudyard Kipling's fictional character, he was born in India where his father, St. John Philby, who had "gone native," was part of the Indian civil service. The father, a noted scholar and adventurer, sided with colonial peoples against the British Empire. There has been considerable speculation that this was the root cause of "Kim's" disloyalty. Though the elder Philby may have been antiestablishment, he sent Kim to the most establishment of institutions— first, his father's old school, Westminster, and then on to Cambridge, which in the early 1930s harbored many Communists. Communism was fashionable at the good schools then.

In 1934 Philby married an Austrian Communist, Litzi Kohlmann, in Vienna. At this time he received instructions from Soviet Intelligence to return to Britain and build a new right-wing life. So he returned, joined the Nazi-tinged Anglo-German fellowship, and shortly shipped out to Spain as a journalist to report the Civil War from the Franco side. Though he was not then a regular *Times* employee, some of his pro-Franco pieces appeared in that paper.

After Franco's victory in 1939, Philby soon went to France to report World War II for the *Times;* when the British had to withdraw from the Continent he returned to England. With help from his friend Guy Burgess (also a Soviet agent, see below) he got a job at the facetiously named Guy Fawkes College, which trained agents in propaganda techniques for Section D of MI-6, shortly to become part of Special Operations Executive (SOE). He did well during the war and by 1945 he was the head of all British Intelligence activities against Soviet espionage and in line to head MI-6. What a coup for Soviet Intelligence! In the late 1940s Philby, by then representing MI-6 in Washington, helped plan the Anglo-American operation, sending hundreds of agents into Communist Albania. Thanks to Philby's tip, the Albanians caught and executed nearly all of these agents. When both Maclean and Burgess fled to the Soviet Union, Philby came under suspicion to the extent that J. Edgar Hoover of the FBI would no longer deal with him. Philby was recalled and sacked, but in the mid-1950s, MI-6 set him up as a journalist working out of Lebanon. In 1962 a KGB man defected and told the British that there had been a Soviet agent within MI-6 until the early 1950s; suspicions again fell on Kim and he fled to Moscow. "I have come home," he declared from Moscow. The grateful Soviets awarded him the Order of the Red Banner, "for outstanding services over many years."

2. GUY BURGESS (1910–1963)

Those less generous than I have branded Burgess a psychopath. Burgess was an utterly decadent, flamboyant, homosexual Soviet spy within British Intelligence and the Foreign Office during the 1930s and '40s. Having attended Eton and the Naval College at Dartmouth in 1930, he went up to Cambridge where he studied history and met Anthony Blunt, Donald Maclean, and Kim Philby. He roomed with Blunt and helped recruit enthusiastic Communists for Soviet Intelligence. In 1935, he began a career as a British Broadcasting

Corporation journalist but continued to act as a contact and courier for Soviet Intelligence, particularly with agents like John Cairncross at the Foreign Office and Philby then in Spain.

In 1939, Burgess joined Section D of MI-6, which was undergoing tremendous expansion. It was he who facetiously named the Section D school for dirty tricks and propaganda "Guy Fawkes College" after the central figure in the 1605 plot to blow up Parliament. Sometime in 1941, Burgess apparently went back to spending most of his time at the BBC, but then in 1944 he went full time to the Foreign Office, where he used his access to secret documents to keep the Russians well informed. In 1950, he was sent to the United States as second secretary at the embassy in Washington. Conveniently, Kim Philby had the cover position of first secretary. Burgess even moved into Philby's home as a boarder.

Later Philby claimed in his memoirs that he was the one who tipped off Burgess that Maclean was under suspicion. This should be seen as just another of the numerous whoppers in Philby's memoirs, obviously designed to divert suspicion from some other Soviet mole within the British Intelligence establishment. Blunt made the escape connection with the Russians, but Blunt himself could not bear to leave his cushy life in England. Though he was ordered to escape with Burgess and Maclean, he stayed behind when they bolted for Russia in 1951.

Never was there a poorer fit between an exile and his adoptive land than Burgess and the USSR. His hosts hated homosexuals, and, being very patriotic themselves, were always suspicious of traitors. His London wit and upper-class accent meant nothing in the workers' paradise. The vain and urbane sophisticate who loved to mock the rubes was himself shown to be an ignorant rube in the great game. In his depression, and often wearing his old school tie, he drank himself to death in a dozen years.

3. DONALD MACLEAN (1913–1983)

Donald Maclean started at Cambridge in 1931, where he became involved in the Communist Party and in Soviet espionage. Soviet Intelligence files opened in the early 1990s indicate that Philby recruited Maclean into Soviet Intelligence. After publicly repudiating Communism, he got an appointment in the British Foreign Office in 1934. For the next 10 years, he reported everything of interest to the Russians. In 1944, Maclean was appointed first secretary at the British Embassy in Washington, D.C.

Over the next four years, his reports to the Russians included the wonders of Anglo-American atomic science and the super-secret meeting to set up the North Atlantic Treaty Organization (NATO). No one in the American or British public had a clue about these negotiations, but Joe Stalin in Moscow was fully briefed. By passing on to the Soviets and their Chinese friends the news that the United States would not use atomic weapons, or push for a decisive victory, or invade China, the Communist side was able to fight an almost risk-free war in Korea.

The tension of Maclean's spy work apparently exacerbated his drinking and reckless behavior, so he was recalled and reassigned. First, he was sent to Egypt, where he was also out of control, and then to the American desk at the Foreign Office in London. Unfortunately for Maclean the American Venona code-

Marvin Greene/© 1964 Plain Dealer

When this photo was taken in 1964, John Cairncross was head of
the Romance Languages Department at Western Reserve
University (now Case Western Reserve University) in Cleveland.
From the 1930s through the early 1950s, he had been one of the
Soviet Union's most important spies in the British government.
Among other things, he gave the Soviets their first news of the atom
bomb project.

breaking operation had revealed a Soviet agent in the Foreign Office, and as the investigation closed in someone tipped Maclean and Burgess. The London headlines soon read: "DIPLOMATS MISSING."

4. SIR ANTHONY BLUNT (1907–1983)

The son of an Anglican clergyman on the edges of the aristocracy, Blunt spent several of his early years in Paris where his father served as chaplain to the British Embassy. After public school, Blunt went to Cambridge where he became a fellow of Trinity College in 1932. As mentioned above he also became a Communist at Cambridge and met his new friends Philby, Burgess, Maclean, and John Cairncross. In 1937, he took a trip to the Soviet Union to examine the Workers' Paradise at first hand. He must have been given a good snow job because Blunt returned an even more ardent devotee of the Soviet system.

One of Blunt's MI-5 jobs was to read the contents of diplomatic bags of other countries (the Brits did this routinely). He passed to the Soviets all the choicest morsels. At the end of the war, he even told a superior of the great pleasure he took in giving the Soviets the name of every MI-5 officer. Only a person in the club and of Blunt's class could have said this without any consequences as he did. Blunt remained the Surveyor of the Queen's Pictures for nearly 20 years after MI-5, and MI-6 knew he had been a long-term Soviet spy. The explanation is that at the end of World War II Blunt, then in MI-5, went with the royal archivist on a secret mission to Germany to retrieve certain potentially embarrassing correspondence between the Royal family and their German Hesse cousins. (The British Royal family are Germans who had a very German family name, Coberg-Saxe-Gotha, until the anti-German frenzy of World War I when they took the name of their castle—Windsor.)

5. THE FIFTH MAN REVEALED—FINALLY, JOHN CAIRNCROSS (1913-1995)

Though it is clear from reading Cairncross's FBI file that they knew him to be a Soviet agent in early 1964, the public was not sure until 1990. Then a Soviet defector, Oleg Gordievsky, blew his cover and Cairncross, then living in France, finally publicly confirmed it, as he had done for the FBI in Cleveland in 1964. Intelligence writers can be forever grateful for his years of silence. Several had made a good living speculating in print on the Fifth Man. It must be said that Barrie Penrose and David Leitch had got it right in a *Sunday Times* piece in 1979.

Cairncross, a brilliant language student, had been spotted at Cambridge by Anthony Blunt and recruited by James Klugman. He was told by the Soviets to join the Foreign Office in 1936. By 1940, he was secretary to Lord Hankey, who chaired a whole slew of very secret committees, including that on building an atomic bomb. This was the Soviets' first tip on the bomb. From Hankey, Cairncross went to Bletchley Park, a country estate where the British were decoding and reading the messages generated by the German Enigma cipher machine.

6. FROM RECTORY TO MONASTERY VIA TREACHERY—WILLIAM JOHN CHRISTOPHER VASSALL (1924-1996)

In 1954 Vassall, the son of a prominent British clergyman, went to Russia as a clerk at the British Embassy.

There he attended a homosexual party the Soviets had arranged for him. He got drunk and ended up as he said "in a complicated array of sexual activities with a number of different men." The ever-thoughtful Soviets photographed these memorable moments, and Mr. Vassall was on the hook.

Moving back to Britain, Vassall found employment with various branches of the Admiralty including the Naval Intelligence Division, where he was so trusted that he was able to simply take documents home in his *Times*. His spying went on for seven years. Nobody seemed to check on how a 14-pound-a-week clerk lived in a 10-pound-a-week flat on Dolphin Square, London, or wore Saville Row suits (he had 19 of them). In the end, it appears that Mr. Vassall may have been a victim—a discard—used by the Soviets to enhance the bona fides of some higher agent in British Intelligence. That most likely candidate is Roger Hollis, then head of MI-5, who was made to look good by the capture of Vassall and who has long been suspected of being a Soviet agent.

7. THE GRANDFATHER MOLE—GUY LIDDELL (d. 1958)

This topic opens a whole can of worms since the sad fact is that few Soviet agents were caught during the Cold War compared with the actual number cavorting around in America, England, and Western Europe. For example, estimates are that the Soviets had 300 to 1,000 illegals in the field at any one time during the Cold War. But there are also a number of British Intelligence officials, some even higher than Philby who had all the markings of Soviet agents. One of these was Guy Liddell, deputy director-general of MI-5 from 1947 to 1952. He has vied with Roger Hollis, the head of MI-

5, as the suspected top Soviet mole within the British Intelligence establishment.

As the mole hunters have pointed out, Liddell brought Hollis, Graham Mitchell (another suspect), Blunt, and Tomas Harris into MI-5, and with the help of Blunt and Harris, brought Burgess and Philby into MI-6. If one is known by one's friends, Liddell looks suspicious. The late John Costello, in *Mask of Treachery*, lists some 21 puzzling failures and screw-ups on Liddell's watch. One is left with the conclusion that he was unbelievably unlucky, criminally incompetent, or very believably traitorous—"The grandfather" Soviet mole in Costello's words.

8. THE TUNNEL TATTLING ESCAPE ARTIST (1923–)

George Blake, born Georg Behar in the Netherlands, was 18 years old when the Germans invaded in 1940. He was interned, but escaped. He then joined the Dutch resistance, but German counterintelligence identified him and he had to escape across occupied France and the Pyrenees into Spain, and finally on to Britain. In Britain, he joined Special Operations Executive. By the end of World War II, he was with British Naval Intelligence. He then transferred to the Foreign Office and was sent to South Korea in 1947. In 1950, the invading North Korean Communists captured him.

In a rare failure, he did not escape from the Communists. Either he was a victim, brainwashed by the Commies, or he genuinely shifted loyalties. At any rate, he returned a Communist, joined MI-6, and was sent to Berlin where he told the Soviets about the Berlin Tunnel that MI-6 and the CIA had burrowed into East Berlin to tap into Russian communications. He also whiled away the hours turning in Western agents behind the Iron Curtain. They were never heard from again. However, Berlin was a very tricky place for a double agent; there were so many agents, double agents, buyouts, sellouts, and defectors. Blake transferred to Lebanon. Alas, a defector from the East did blow his cover. MI-6 lured him back to London and arrested him. The Brits said that Blake had blown at least 40 Western agents. Years later Blake wrote of this like a retired gunfighter of the old West. He had lost count of the bodies—400, 500, 600—he did not know anymore. He got a 42-year sentence, but he escaped from London's Wormwood Scrubs Prison in 1966 after serving only six years. He made his way to Moscow to a job in the British section of the KGB. Quite a record. One published photograph shows Blake and Philby and their Russian wives at Blake's dacha. The number of liquor bottles, both empty and full, on the table suggests that all were well fortified against the slings and arrows of life.

9.   TO THE SOUTH SLAVS WITH PERFIDY (1912–1977)

James Klugman is not nearly as well known as the others, but he certainly was as successful. None of the others described can be said to have turned a country over to the Communists, in this case Yugoslavia. Short and flabby, Klugman had been a "clever oddity" at Gresham School in Norfolk. He won a scholarship to Trinity College, Cambridge, where he was a flaming Communist missionary. He even had a major Communist Party meeting of Oxbridge, London School of Economics, and University College, London student Communists at his parents' home over the Easter holidays in 1932. How a blatant Communist like Klugman became deputy director of SOE's Yugoslavian section remains unclear. Some say it is because his records were destroyed in a bombing raid, but so many in the narrow confines of the British establishment knew him, and he was so blatant, that this explanation seems far-fetched. It is now clear from SOE documents that Klugman systematically faked and manipulated reports from Yugoslavia so that Allied support was withdrawn from the pro-Western guerrillas of General Mihailovic and given to the Communist Tito, who had collaborated with Hitler according to writer Michael Lees.

10. STILL UNREPENTANT AFTER ALL THESE YEARS—MRS. MELITA NORWOOD (1912–   )

The KGB recruited this dedicated British Communist as a spy in 1937. She was secretary for something called the British Non-Ferrous Metals Association, which was evidently the cover for "Tube Alloys," the British project to build an atom bomb and do other nuclear research. For 40 years, she gave the Soviets everything she could on British atomic research. For this she received money and in 1958 the "Order of the Red Banner." No one would have known about this had not KGB archivist Vasili Mitrokhin defected in 1992, bringing with him hundreds of pages of notes and hundreds of names of KGB agents—Norwood's among them. But neither Norwood nor any of the other hundreds of agents named by Mitrokhin were ever prosecuted. The official British report on this failure to prosecute by MI-5 has that sort of vague feel that one gets when looking at MI-5 efforts, or lack of efforts, to catch Philby, Burgess, Maclean, and Blunt.

"The Security service [MI-5] denied that any decision was taken not to prosecute Mrs. Norwood. However, the Committee believes that a member of staff, to all intents and purposes, took the decision. By deciding not to interview Mrs. Norwood at this time and making no attempt to gain evidence that would support a prosecution effectively prevented her possible prosecution." News of Norwood's guilt did not leak until 1999 when a BBC reporter tracked her down from clues in the censored copy of the documents he had obtained. When interviewed, she readily admitted her guilt. This certainly justified her KGB job evaluation as a "committed, reliable and disciplined agent, striving to be of the utmost assistance."

Her commitment and simple belief in the Soviet Union sound like those of the academic intelligentsia in the 1920s and '30s. At a press conference outside her Bexleyheath, southeast London home, she said: "I did what I did not to make money but to help prevent the defeat of a new system which had, at great cost, given ordinary people food and fares which they could afford, a good education and health service." No mention here of the Kulaks, the purges, tens of millions or perhaps 100 million deaths perpetrated by the "new system."

Loyalty, Loyalty, Wherefore Art Thou Loyalty?

While it is certainly true that Soviet Intelligence has had great success in penetrating to the highest reaches of Western intelligence, the West has had its successes also. But, it must also be recognized that many of these agents were not so much cultivated as grudgingly accepted after they threw themselves at Western intelligence agencies. A number had to be very persistent to get the West to accept their gifts. Critics trace some of this lack of success to Soviet moles within their services.

1. "... NO ATTAINDER OF TREASON SHALL WORK CORRUPTION OF BLOOD ..."

says the United States Constitution. Basically, this means the children of the treasonous shall not suffer for the sins of their parents. The Founding Fathers of the United States were students of history, and they wrote this because "corruption of blood" had worked much mischief in England over the centuries. The Russians obeyed no such rule and GRU Colonel Oleg Penkovsky found his career stymied because his father had died fighting the Reds in the Russian civil war in 1919. To get even, he became a double agent. The published record of his exploits is stunning—over 10,000 pages of secret Soviet documents photographed and delivered to the West and another 1,000–1,500 pages of debriefing transcripts. An American intelligence man who professed to have worked on them once told me that the "Penkovsky Papers," fill a filing cabinet. "You wouldn't believe the stuff that's there," I remember him saying.

Though running Penkovsky was a joint CIA/MI-6 project, neither recruited him. He was more like a teenager who just cannot take no for an answer. His bold, almost crazy, overtures in 1960 frightened Western intelligence agencies worried about provocateurs. In the spring of 1961, the Brits finally took a chance. Penkovsky was in London heading a delegation seeking Western technology. What could the Brits lose on their own turf? In a standard setup, Western intelligence had taken rooms in his hotel, the Mount Royal. For several weeks during that spring of 1961 he came down to their rooms, drank wine, and gushed information all night. His information, its range, and its depth were stunning. The Soviet nuclear and missile programs were not nearly ready, but they were readying their civil defense program to survive a nuclear war. He delivered everything from the Kremlin telephone directory (giving the West its first real grip on the Russian chain of command) to the names of Soviet Intelligence officers working in the West. There seems no unclassified convincing explanation of how Penkovsky's cover was blown. Good cases can be made for a mole or moles in

Western intelligence and Penkovsky's own reckless-ness. At any rate, the Soviets apparently threw him alive into a crematorium—after a fair trial, of course.

2. CODE NAME: JESSANT—THE GIFT HORSE REJECTED AND SORT OF ACCEPTED

Here we have another example not of the U.S./U.K. in-telligence services seducing KGB operatives, but of fighting off volunteer defectors from the KGB or so withholding their information as to greatly lessen its usefulness. Jessant (originally called Gunner) is the British code name for Vasili Mitrokhin, the chief archi-vist of the KGB's records. He had worked for the KGB's First Chief Directorate from 1948 to 1984. He defected to the British in 1992, bringing with him thousands of pages of secret KGB files. Mitrokhin first tried to give this material to the Americans but they were either dead asleep at the switch and, perhaps frightened by the McCarthyite implications, sent him away. Perhaps with good reason—the American Chapter, only one of 10, consisted of more than 800 densely typed pages. There were also 27 envelopes and 107 exercise books of contemporaneous notes. Just one of the envelopes contained the names of 645 KGB agents and contacts. (The names of 300 agents in France were eventually passed on to that country.)

Even the British did not seem too anxious to touch Mr. Mitrokhin when he first appeared at the British Em-bassy in a Baltic state on March 24, 1992. They told him to come back in two weeks. He did, and things were off and rolling, very slowly. Eventually MI-6 was to describe the material as: "a case of exceptional counter-intelligence significance . . . promising to nul-lify many of Russia's current assets." Even the American FBI, when finally given a look, said the material is: "the most detailed and extensive pool of CI (counter-intelligence) ever received by the FBI." Mitrokhin wanted to publish his material and it did eventually produce *The Mitrokhin Archive*, but that was seven years later in 1999. Moreover, it was thoroughly censored to keep British government embarrassment to a minimum. (One condition of publication set by the British government was that no names appear unless that name had already been made public or the person prosecuted.) Mitrokhin was very unhappy with the product and told the British that he had not accomplished what he set out to achieve, because he had lost control of the material. Not one prosecution came from all these names of agents, even after an enterprising BBC reporter ferreted out the name of a spy in Britain's atom project, Melita Norwood, who admitted spying for the Soviets and who said she would do it again. With all the fumbling and bumbling, it is easy to see why specialists suspect that the moles that have been found in the United States/Britain are like the visible parts of a tree—half of its wood is underground.

3. THE GRASS IS JUST AS DISLOYAL ON THE OTHER SIDE OF THE FENCE—THE NAZIS

The Nazis had far more than their share of intelligence failures and enemies within. For starters, there was the "unbreakable" Enigma cipher, which by the early war years the Brits were breaking so rapidly they often read the messages before the German military commanders to whom they were addressed. The ruthlessly efficient Nazis of movie and TV fame were easy marks when compared to the Soviets. The Brits captured and turned every agent Hitler had in England, while swarms of Soviet agents penetrated every level of British and American society and government. While counterintelligence seems to have been an afterthought for the Germans, the KGB lived to find spies and secret wreckers.

4. TREASON AT THE TOP—ADMIRAL CANARIS AND THE BLACK ORCHESTRA

Admiral Wilhelm Canaris, a conservative who hated Hitler and the Nazis, was the head of German military intelligence—the Abwehr—from 1935 until early 1944 when Hitler had it disbanded. Hitler had Canaris executed for conspiring against him. Hitler was surely correct; apparently the admiral had also secretly collaborated with the British and Americans. Canaris sent secret messages to the British and French telling them to oppose Hitler's moves into Austria and Czechoslovakia in 1938 and Poland in 1939. Only the Polish request was honored, thus bringing on World War II. Both the good admiral and his director of sabotage, Erwin von Lahousen, tried to hamper the military operations they planned.

5. THE REAL KICK-OFF TO THE COLD WAR

Igor Gouzenko, an officer in Soviet military intelligence, worked in Canada under cover as a cipher clerk in the Soviet Embassy in Ottawa. His harrowing defection with his pregnant wife and young child and a well-chosen collection of secret Soviet documents took place in early September 1945. Some scholars point to this defection as the beginning of the Cold War. Others suggest that Gouzenko's documents and testimony simply exposed the fact that the Soviets had long been running a serious espionage war against the West.

At any rate, the Canadians thought Gouzenko "too

hot a potato" and were loath to take him in. Canadian Prime Minister Mackenzie King wrote in his diary that suicide might be Gouzenko's best course of action. To the rescue came the Canadian Sir William Stephenson (Intrepid), the wartime head of British Intelligence in the United States who threw his influence behind the defector's cause. Gouzenko's evidence blew the lid off the Soviet atom bomb espionage and led to the arrest of Klaus Fuchs and Alan Nunn May. It also added to the mounting testimony against U.S. Treasury official Harry Dexter White and State Department official Alger Hiss.

6. GOOD GIRL GOES TO THE FBI

From 1938 to 1944 Elizabeth Bentley had been a Soviet Intelligence courier for her lover Jacob Golos. This work included carrying lots of documents snatched by Soviet agents in the U.S. government. Unfortunately for the Soviets Golos died suddenly in late 1943; the Soviets took away many of Bentley's duties leaving her isolated and alone, with no one to talk to. So in 1945 Bentley talked to the FBI about her adventures. She had no documents, but the FBI was able to confirm much of what she said, and the broken Soviet codes of the Venona project also backed her up. In 1948 she told much of her story to congressional committees. She named names, including White House assistant Lauchlin Currie, and once again, Treasury official Harry Dexter White.

7. WHITTAKER CHAMBERS MAKES RICHARD nixon

One of those Bentley named as involved in the Soviet underground was Whittaker Chambers, a senior editor for *Time* magazine. From 1934 to 1939 Chambers had also been a courier for those stealing documents in Washington. As for many Communists, the Nazi-Soviet Pact of August 1939 brought on a crisis of conscience. He went to Assistant Secretary of State Adolph Berle and told him that his assistant Alger Hiss was a Communist agent. Berle then thought this a crazy charge. When Chambers and Bentley repeated these charges before the House Un-American Activities Committee in July 1948 they caused a sensation. Hiss denied the charges.

Chambers had withheld and hidden a number of documents in a pumpkin on his farm. An obscure member of the committee, Richard Nixon, was tipped to these documents and got a subpoena for them. The widely circulated photograph of Nixon peering through a magnifying glass at the "pumpkin papers" made him an instant celebrity. He parlayed this fame into a nomination for vice president in 1950 and president in 1960 and 1968. As for Hiss, he went to jail for perjury.

8.   A FULL CLEVELAND

When Soviet Intelligence officer Aleksandr Orlov died in the 1990s in Lakewood, Ohio, a Cleveland suburb, it was revealed that he had been living quietly in the Cleveland area for decades. He was one of the highest ranking Soviet Intelligence officers ever to defect to the West. His resume was impressive. Orlov had run the Cambridge spy ring—Philby, Burgess et al.—during the 1930s. He had been the NKVD resident in Spain in the later 1930s and had, among other services to Stalin, stolen the Spanish gold supply, loaded it on a boat and sent it to Russia. Shortly thereafter he received an order to return to the Soviet Union.

National Security Agency

This picture was taken at a 1948 congressional hearing.
The woman second from the left is Elizabeth Bentley, the
onetime Soviet courier turned FBI informant. Third from the
left is Whittaker Chambers, an editor for *Time* and also a
confessed Soviet agent. Closest to the camera is former State
Department official and Soviet spy Alger Hiss. Chambers's
public accusations led to Hiss's downfall.

This was the time of the Great Purges and Orlov
decided, probably wisely, since he was the only witness
to numerous Soviet dirty deeds, that returning was not
a good idea. He secretly took his family first to Canada
and then to the United States. He also sent a letter to
Stalin swearing loyalty and saying that he had stashed
packets of very damaging documents in a number of
places and that these would be released if anything
happened to him. The deal was that if Orlov and his
family remained safe, so would Stalin's dirty secrets.
Orlov seems to have kept his side of the bargain. He

never gave away any major secrets even after the FBI discovered and questioned him.

9. BORIS MORROS, THE HOLLYWOOD MOVIEMAKER

Boris Morros was a successful movie producer with credits for films such as *Second Chorus* with Fred Astaire and *Flying Deuces* with Laurel and Hardy. In the 1930s he was also having trouble sending packages to his parents in the Soviet Union. A Soviet Intelligence officer, Edward Herbert, appeared and said he could help. The officer, of course, also wanted help and Morros supplied him with credentials as his talent scout in Germany. In 1942 the agent reappeared and told Morros to forget the name Herbert, that he was Vassiliy Zarubin, a Soviet official who would see that Morros's aged father came to the United States in return for using Morros's film company as a cover. In 1943 FBI surveillance of Zarubin revealed that Morros was working for Soviet Intelligence. In 1947 the FBI confronted Morros and he agreed to become a double agent, a role he continued for a decade, blowing the cover of numerous Soviet agents.

10. THE HIGHEST LAST, LIEUTENANT GENERAL DIMITRI POLYAKOV

Soviet Intelligence loved to make home movies. Episode 24 of Ted Turner's CNN *Cold War* series covers spying. It opens with footage of Lieutenant General Dimitri Polyakov in a headlock, to keep him from taking poison, as he is being arrested. Polyakov was the highest ranking GRU officer ever to work for American intelligence. Under the code name Top Hat the FBI began running him in 1962. Reports are that the United States received invaluable intelligence on everything from biological warfare to missile developments from him. Unfortunately Polyakov was one of the two dozen U.S. agents sold to Soviet Intelligence by Aldrich Ames for $2.7 million. Even more unfortunately for him, he was among the 10 who were executed.

Ten for the Intelligence Cognoscenti

The following 10 items have recently been declassified or remain so hidden that even insiders in intelligence have probably not heard of them. You may note
a lack of civilian control of the intelligence apparatus
in some countries at some moments in history or the
bending to the will of the greatest power. I did not
promise to tell the reader how things should be, but
how they have really happened. The fact is that sometimes the civilian leadership of some countries could
not know, were not trusted, or did not want to know.

Politicians have fundamental values—getting and
staying elected, cowardice—that are sometimes at
variance with the values of their intelligence agencies—
protecting hard won secrets and the hope of getting future secrets, protecting the nation. In one instance
someone in the White House even wished to protect
Soviet Intelligence or its agents in the United States.
Several of these items involve Ferret electronic surveillance flights, which surveyed, among other things, the
Soviet radar network. The most amazing and secret
truth was that there was no Soviet radar network over

the Northern sector of the USSR during the 1950s and only a spotty system later. There was hardly any radar between the port of Murmansk on the west and Alaska on the east. The United States could have attacked the Soviet Union at any time without the Soviets having any warning.

1. THE LITTLE MERMAID AND THE FERRET

In the early 1950s the U.S. Air Force attaché in Denmark made an agreement with the head of the Danish Defense Intelligence Service, Colonel Hans Mathiesen, to allow "Ferret" electronic surveillance aircraft to secretly overfly Denmark on their way to cruise the Baltic Iron Curtain coast. This evaded the messy problems of gaining consent or even telling the civilian Danish government. The secret documents say that there were "security considerations," which prevented this disclosure—a nice way of saying that the civilian government could not be trusted.

2. KNOW NOTHING, SAY NOTHING—THE CASE OF TURKEY

The first American sites for electronic surveillance of the Soviet Union from Turkey were unknown to that country's civilian authorities. There was a secret agreement between the U.S. military men on the ground in Turkey and the head of the Turkish General Staff. The only problems came in making sure that Washington officials did not inadvertently start talking about this arrangement with Turkish politicians or diplomats who knew nothing of it.

3. STANLEY BALDWIN BABBLES

At dawn on May 12, 1927, several hundred police and British Intelligence agents swarmed into 49 Moorgate, the London offices of ARCOS, the Soviet Trading Company. ARCOS was also a cover for and center of Soviet espionage and subversion in Great Britain with a staff of more than 300, far more than could be justified by the small amount of trade between Great Britain and the USSR.

This was in fact a copy of a raid that the Chinese had pulled the previous month on the Soviet Trading Company in Peking. Both raids yielded a trove of evidence of espionage. The London raiders found a vault in the basement and after forcing the door found two men and a woman busily burning documents. There were valuable documents not yet in the flames—lists of agents, their addresses, letter boxes, and copies of secret British government documents. Unfortunately the exact documents that they were searching for were not found. Only later was a secret exit found where they might have been spirited away. The Baldwin government was furious and threw the Soviets out. None were allowed to enter the country for two years.

The real disaster came when the friends of the Soviets in Parliament ignored the evidence found, raised a ruckus about the raid, and demanded to see more evidence about why the raid had been conducted. Prime Minister Stanley Baldwin caved in and produced evidence that could have been gained only if the British were able to read the Soviet codes. This, of course, did not get Baldwin's Parliamentary enemies off his neck—scoring political points had always been their goal, but it did alert the Soviets to their code security problem. They went to onetime pads and British Intelligence was not able to read a word for almost two decades. Another result was that when the British later penetrated the German and Japanese codes, MI-6 insisted that as few chatty, cowardly politicians know of it as possible.

4.   INSUBORDINATION I—KILL THE BRIDE

The first cover name for the Venona project was Bride. These names denote a World War II era project to read Soviet ciphered messages between the United States and Moscow Center. Though the messages were in supposedly unbreakable onetime pad ciphers the Soviets had, in the shortage conditions of war, used some onetime pages two or more times. The American code breakers at Arlington Hall near Washington spotted this duplication and started reading these messages. Someone at the White House, probably Lauchlin Currie, senior administrative assistant to President Roosevelt and a Soviet Intelligence collaborator with the Soviet cover name Page, gave orders to stop work on Soviet ciphers. The OSS technically obeyed White House and State Department orders (see Operation Stella Polaris in item 5) and turned over to the Soviets material on their codes they had received from Finnish sources.

OSS also played the game by not establishing a Russian desk. Colonel Clarke at Arlington Hall informed his subordinates that he had been told by the White House to stop Bride/Venona, but they were to ignore this order. The project went on to reveal the enormous Soviet penetration of the atom bomb project, the U.S. Treasury, the U.S. State Department, the OSS, and even the White House—more than 350 Soviet agents, collaborators and informants, and Currie himself. It confirmed the revelations of onetime Soviet agents Elizabeth Bentley and Whittaker Chambers. One need only sit down with a few hundred of these decrypted messages to understand the massiveness of the Soviet effort.

5. INSUBORDINATION II—OPERATION STELLA POLARIS

Tiny Finland surprised everyone in the fall of 1939 and the early months of 1940 as it turned back the brunt of repeated Soviet military attacks. Some of this success was based on impressive SIGINT capability, and when the Finns evacuated their records and key personnel, Operation Stella Polaris, to Sweden in 1944, they had hopes of continuing. The Swedes would not allow this and as host, the Swedes claimed most of the goodies.

National Security Agency

Arlington Hall, a junior college for women in Arlington, Virginia, was taken over by the Army Signal Intelligence Corps early in World War II. It was here that the theoretically unbreakable Soviet one-time pads were successfully attacked through the Venona project.

The Finn in charge, Major Hallamaa, then auctioned off the leftovers and those rich Americans bought much and paid well—200,000 Crowns for a 1941 five-digit Soviet military code, for example. Being a compassionate man and not wishing to see any bidder disappointed, Major Hallamaa sold a copy of this to the British for half price—100,000 Crowns, and to then sold it the French the Japanese each according to ability to pay. He then retired to Spain to grow carnations. The French purchased lists of some 95 Russian codes broken or captured and perhaps another 25 codes of the NKVD (later KGB) and the Red Army Headquarters codes. This was certainly a bonanza for any code breaker. Colonel William Donovan at OSS was told by the White House and State Department to give these materials back to our Russian allies. Donovan, not being as innocent or perhaps as treasonous as those above him, complied with orders, but made copies for the U.S. Army code breakers, among others. This was completely off the books; neither the CIA nor the NSA can find records of receiving these copies. However, in the National Security Collection of documents on Venona there remain 150 pages in Finnish. Just teasing leftovers from the disappeared Stella Polaris.

6.   FIVE WHO DIED FOR SIGINT SECURITY

The bureaucratic word for the effort to capture and read another country's coded messages is SIGINT, which stands for signals intelligence. The secret ability to read a foreign country's codes and thus enhance the security of the code breakers' own country can make a few lives expendable. In addition, talkative politicians are often seen as the weak link. In 1975, Australian Signals Intelligence read a message from the Indonesian military saying they intended to kill five Australian journalists covering the Indonesian invasion of East Timor. High officials of the Signals Intelligence agency feared that if they told Prime Minister Gough Whitlam he would talk or send some sort of warning that would reveal to the Indonesians that the Aussies were reading their secret messages. The Indonesians would then change their codes or worse, their code system, thus blinding Australian Intelligence. Signals Intelligence withheld the information. The five journalists were killed. Stanley Baldwin's confession to Parliament about the ARCOS raid still hangs heavily over the guardians of SIGINT three-quarters of a century later.

7. THAT THE GUILTY GO FREE—ONE PRICE OF VENONA

The Venona decrypting project was a powerful tool of the FBI and its allies in the 1940s and 1950s. A number of Soviet spy rings in Great Britain, Australia, and the United States were disrupted using this information. However, U.S. Intelligence seldom risked Venona in courts of law. More than 200 Soviet agents were identified, but only 15 were ever prosecuted for fear of blowing Venona's cover in an open court of law. For examples, Judith Coplon was a Soviet spy in the Justice Department but charges against her had to be dropped because the compelling evidence against her was in Venona. William Weisband was a Russian-born American Signals Intelligence expert, but also a Soviet spy. The great evidence against him was in Venona, which could not be chanced in court. He was sentenced to a year in jail in 1950 for contempt for failing to answer questions about his pre–World War II membership in the Communist Party. This fear of disclosing the extent of Venona allowed the American and European leftists and the media to portray these trials as witch hunts and to strongly suggest that the idea of Communist agents in the U.S. government was largely the product of right-wing paranoia and irrational fears. One does not hear this sort of thing today.

8. PRINTING PRESS MONEY

"George [Bowden] arranged, through Westbrook Steele, director of the Institute of Paper Chemistry, Appleton, Wisconsin, to have the Paper Institute manufacture paper for forged passports and for the paper on which German Marks were printed. The Marks flooded Axis countries and caused considerable financial problems." This is from a letter concerning OSS official George Bowden from his wife (also OSS) to Ernest Cuneo, World War II liaison between British Intelligence, the White House, the FBI, the Treasury, and the Justice Department.

9. PLOWING UP ANIMAL FARM

One of the CIA's great assets in Hollywood was an agent named Carlton Alsop who, by the 1950s, was working at Paramount. He made regular reports about Communists on the celluloid scene and on his success at planting patriotic ideas in movies. Shortly after the death of George Orwell (real name Eric Blair) in 1950 our old friend Howard Hunt sent Alsop and a onetime Hollywood writer Finis Farr to England to buy the film rights to *Animal Farm* from Orwell's widow. For a proper sum of money and a chance to meet movie star Clark Gable, the widow signed over the rights. Says Hunt in his memoir: "From this was to come the animated cartoon film of Orwell's *Animal Farm* which the

National Security Agency

Judith Coplon was caught passing Justice Department documents to Soviet Intelligence in 1949. The problem for prosecutors was that the evidence exposing her was from Venona. Her case was eventually dropped when government officials could not figure out a way to continue her prosecution without compromising the super-secret Venona project.

CIA financed and distributed throughout the world." This was a Cadillac operation—one of the most ambitious animated features of its day. Though critics noticed that the ending was changed to put all the blame on the Communist look-alike pigs at least you could still recognize the story—a condition not always true in Hollywood's translation of books to film.

10. 1984 ACCORDING TO THE CIA

Once again Howard Hunt came to the fore. He talked the owner of the rights to *1984* into cooperating, got the financing, and pushed the film along. Sol Stein, the director of a CIA front called the American Committee for Cultural Freedom, gave advice freely, including a more optimistic ending. His ending was not used, but in an early precursor to *Clue,* two different endings were made—one for the European audience and one for the Americans. Both these Orwell films, though needing some tweaking, fit with the CIA's militant Cold War theme of the evils of totalitarian Communism and the need to be ready to fight it.

Ten for Tube Alloys and the Manhattan Project

In the early 1990s the Russians admitted they had ten agents stealing the secrets from the U.S./U.K. project to build an atomic bomb in the 1940s. They seem to have been divided into two groups though even today the details of tradecraft are unclear. The Soviet penchant for running two or more parallel spy groups isolated from one another had at least three purposes: for security—if one cell was blown, the others remained; to backstop one another; and to check on one another to prevent stunts like the British Double Cross Committee pulled on the Nazis. Given the tight security on the Enormoz project, as the Soviets called the Tube Alloys/ Manhattan project to build the bomb, the Soviet penetration is indeed impressive. The Nazis never came within a whiff of the project. With the exception of Associate Justice of the U.S. Supreme Court Felix Frankfurter, who had his hands in everything, few top American officials had a clue about this project. The secretive and devious President Franklin Roosevelt, a master of intrigue, died in April of 1945. After his swearing-in ceremony Harry Truman was told by the

Secretary of War, Henry Stimson, that when things quieted down he had something to tell him. The something, of course, was the ongoing effort to build a bomb, which was successfully exploded in July. The news flashed to Truman, then at the Potsdam Conference in Germany that, "The Baby is Born." Truman waited for the right moment to tell his "Ally" Joseph Stalin that the United States had discovered a "new weapon of unusual destructive force." Stalin surprised President Truman not by the expected barrage of questions but by his lack of questions. He seemed almost uninterested. It is now obvious that he knew much more about Enormoz than did Truman and had been kept abreast of developments since early 1942. Let's look at those caring and sharing individuals who worked so hard to help the monster, Joseph Stalin, and his monstrous system.

1. A "LEAF" FALLS FOR UNCLE JOE

"Leaf" was the Soviet code name for Donald Maclean, who we talked of elsewhere as one of the Cambridge spies. Maclean who skedaddled to the Soviet Union in 1951 with another old school tie, Burgess. In September 1941 he passed on word to the Soviets that a session of the nuclear advisory committee had met and that British scientists were confident that they could build a uranium bomb in two years. In addition, the Brits were giving top priority to building a uranium-refining factory. John Cairncross, secretary to Lord Hankey, who probably chaired the committee, may have confirmed this. This was the most important news. Even with this forewarning and the complete stealing of the bomb right down to the bolts, it still took the Soviets until 1949 to build the bomb. Had the Soviets been as clueless as President Harry Truman in 1945 it surely would have taken them double or triple this time. Without the bomb Stalin would not have given the North Koreans permission to attack South Korea. However, Soviet spies in the West were determined that their beloved Soviet Union not be at a disadvantage.

2. MORRIS COHEN BEFORE HE BECAME PETER KROGER

Morris Cohen was one of those idealistic 1930s New York Communists who volunteered to fight against the Franco fascists in the Spanish Civil War, thus his reasonable Soviet Intelligence cover name: Volunteer. In 1938, while recuperating from a wound in Barcelona, he was recruited into Soviet Intelligence. Back in New York, he met a physicist acquaintance who told him he had been recruited to work on the project to build the bomb. Cohen recruited this man, who has never been identified, to Soviet Intelligence. The physicist was given the code name "Perseus."

3. LONA COHEN BEFORE SHE BECAME HELEN KROGER

After her husband, Morris, had gone off to the United States Army in early 1943 his faithful wife, who worked in a munitions plant, took over as a Soviet Intelligence courier. Her cover name was Volunteer's Wife. In this capacity she made at least two trips to Albuquerque, New Mexico, to meet with "Perseus" and get secret documents on the atom bomb project. On one of them she was almost caught. The documents were in the bottom of a tissue box but all the train passengers and their parcels were being searched at the train station. She handed the box to the plainclothesman while she

National Security Agency

Atomic scientist and Soviet spy Klaus Fuchs was taken into custody in late 1949 and confessed after a month of interrogation. His confession led authorities to Harry Gold and subsequently David Greenglass and Julius and Ethel Rosenberg.

The trial of Manhattan Project spies Julius and Ethel Rosenberg caused an international sensation. After they were found guilty of espionage, liberals and religious groups at home and abroad protested their impending execution. Many believed that the charges against the couple were fabricated. President Eisenhower refused to grant clemency, and the Rosenbergs were executed in 1953. We now know that the U.S. government was so confident about the verdict because they were reading the Venona decrypts, which confirmed that Julius was a spy and that Ethel was, at the very least, complicit in passing atomic secrets to the Soviets.

got out her ID and ticket. After checking these, he then unknowingly handed the tissue box back to her.

Her luck at this sort of trick was to run out years later when as Helen Kroger she tried to burn her espionage equipment when the British arrested her. At any rate, the Cohens kept at this work until 1950. Then, when the Rosenbergs were arrested, the Cohens disappeared. Probably a good thing—the American public was in a surly mood, what with the Soviets exploding an atom bomb in 1949, the "loss" of China to the Communists, and the soon to be stalemated Korean War. This was also the start of the McCarthy "witch hunts," and if there were no witches we now know that Soviet spies were in good supply. Those caught were unlikely to be treated well. Julius and Ethel Rosenberg went to the electric chair for their atom spying. The Cohens were support staff and runners for this atom spy ring. Julius Rosenberg was paying the Cohens' rent, and when their effects were put into storage, Soviet master spy Colonel Rudolf Abel took care of them. The Cohens, we now know, went to Mexico, then to Moscow, and after further travels emerged in England as antiquarian book dealer Peter Kroger and his wife Helen—support staff for Gordon Lonsdale and the Portland spies stealing naval warfare secrets from the British. The documents the Soviets had supplied the Krogers and their cockamamie cover stories were blown by the fingerprints they had given in the early 1940s when Morris went into the Army and Lona worked in that munitions plant. This explains why they both desperately tried to prevent the Brits from fingerprinting them.

4. HE WAS A SOVIET SPY—JULIUS ROSENBERG

When Julius Rosenberg, cover name Liberal, and his wife Ethel Greenglass Rosenberg were executed in 1953 there were noisy demonstrations in both American and European cities proclaiming their innocence and denouncing American "fascism." Members of the liberal clergy and professorate led the letter-writing campaigns and pro-Rosenberg media blitz. One of the more interesting charges was that of anti-Semitism, neatly ignoring the obvious fact that both the judge and the prosecutor were Jews, drove the prosecution of these poor innocents. The president of France and Pope Pius XII were even persuaded to asked President Eisenhower for clemency for the Rosenbergs. The Rosenbergs, it was said, had been framed by the FBI. The Venona decrypts have confirmed Julius's guilt and, at the very least, Ethel's complicity.

5. THE FAITHFUL AND LOVING WIFE—ETHEL GREENGLASS ROSENBERG

Given the evidence we have today Ethel, cover name Antenna, seems to have been not innocent, but guilty of lesser crimes than her husband Julius. She was a dedicated Communist and wittingly assisted her husband. It also seems obvious that the death sentences for both were used as leverage to try to get one of them to talk, but they continued to protest their innocence.

6. BUZZ FROM THE BUMBLEBEE, THY BROTHER THE TESTIFYER—DAVID GREENGLASS

Trial testimony indicates that Julius and Ethel were already spying for Soviet Intelligence when a windfall and their downfall came their way. In 1944 Ethel's brother David Greenglass, cover name Bumblebee, then in the U.S. Army, was assigned as a machinist to the atom bomb project at Los Alamos, New Mexico. He later testified that the Rosenbergs drew him into their espionage ring and that the ring included scientist Klaus Fuchs, Harry Gold, and the spymaster working out of the Soviet Embassy, Anatoly Yakovlev. This man was indicted along with the Rosenbergs, but he had already left the country and it turned out, in typical Soviet fashion, that the diplomat's name and documents were phony anyway.

Greenglass testified against his sister and brother-in-law and the Rosenberg's supporters responded by savaging him unmercifully. He was smeared as either a liar or a snitch who should have kept his mouth shut. Greenglass provided both material on the trigger mechanism and a rough sketch of the bomb. Critics have pointed out that this sketch was so rough as not to be useful for building a bomb. However, it is good enough to confirm the information coming from others like Klaus Fuchs and "Perseus." Confirmation was always of the utmost importance to the suspicious men in the Kremlin. They were not to be snookered by the "Man Who Never Was," or some smart trick from Britain's Double Cross (XX) Committee. The Soviets were just too well positioned, they had too many agents, collaborators, moles, and agents of influence on too many levels of the U.S. and British governments. There were over 350 in the U.S. government and military according to the parts of the Venona codes that can be read.

7. GOLD THAT TURNED TO DROSS

Harry Gold's work for Soviet Intelligence started in 1935 as he gathered American industrial secrets for them. After the German invasion of the Soviet Union in June of 1941, Gold, under the cover names Goose and Arnold became both a gatherer of information and a major courier to the Soviets. He got rocket and jet research information from Morton Sobell at General Electric Laboratories. His golden sources, however, were in the Manhattan Project. There he worked separately with Klaus Fuchs, a nuclear scientist, and Ethel Rosenberg's brother, David Greenglass. Like an old sweater, the cell came unraveled in 1950 when the British, who had been tipped by the Americans, wooed Fuchs into confessing. Though he did not know Gold's name, he gave enough information that the FBI could track him down. Gold confessed and led to Greenglass, Sobell, and the Rosenbergs. The Cohens, the support staff for all these spies, had to be exfiltrated because they were the tie to Colonel Rudolf Abel, the Soviet illegal who took care of the Cohens' furniture.

8. ANATOLY YATSKOV = ANATOLY YAKOVLEV

As Anatoly Yakovlev this Soviet diplomat was indicted along with the Rosenbergs. However, he had left the United States and was thus never tried. In 1992, he re-emerged as Anatoly Yatskov for an interview with the *Washington Post.* He claimed to the *Post* that the FBI had been able to uncover "only half, perhaps less than half," of the agents he was responsible for in the United States. While admitting to Fuchs, Yatskov said agent "Perseus" was on the job inside the Manhattan Project 18 months before Fuchs. The "father" of the Soviet bomb, Igor Kurchatov, wrote some notes to the Kremlin in March 1943 appraising the material from the atom spies in America. "The receipt of these materials has a huge, invaluable significance for our state and science. . . . Now we have important guidelines for subsequent research that enables us to bypass many laborious phases involved in tackling the uranium problem and reveal new scientific and technical ways of solving it." Even after obtaining complete plans, it took the Soviets four years to build their atom bomb.

9. THE MOLE IN TUBE ALLOYS

Meanwhile, back in England at the British Non-Ferrous Metals Research Association, the home of Tube Alloys, the British atom bomb project, Mrs. Melita Norwood was joyfully handing over to the Soviets everything that came across her desk or into her view. For her efforts, she received among other things an award called "The Order of the Red Banner." After an enterprising reporter tracked Mrs. Norwood down from clues in the expurgated version of the Mitrokhin archive he had been given, there was a considerable government effort to show that little important material was officially available to her.

After all, she was but a lowly secretary. Very logical, very precise, these explanations are full of that tight legal reasoning that passes for logic but is really an effort to evade the issue. "The Order of the Red Banner" is given for bravery in combat or behind enemy lines. It is the same award given to that notoriously effective and valuable Soviet agent Kim Philby. Second, it matters not a whit what material Mrs. Norwood officially had access to. The trick is to be trusted, on the inside— once there, casual conversations, rumors, misdirected papers, a myriad of opportunities fall to any dedicated spy, and all observers say Mrs. Norwood was dedicated. Certainly any businessperson or secretary will find in the government's explanation a chuckle to lighten the day.

10. MLAD COMES UP WITH THE GOODS

"Mlad" was the Soviet Intelligence cover name for Theodore Hall. In a bit of playfulness the Soviets chose the root of the Russian word for "young" as Hall's cover name—he was only 19 years old, a member of the Young Communists League (YCL) and a Harvard undergraduate. He was just the sort of academically brilliant innocent that Soviet Intelligence found such easy marks. This membership in the YCL is not well brought out in CNN's *Cold War* TV series where Hall does confess that he gave the Soviets information on the atom bomb so that the United States would not have a monopoly and put the Soviet Union at a disadvantage. Hall gave them the secret of implosion.

The Company Goes to the Movies

The CIA, often just called "the Company," has been portrayed in many silver screen thrillers. A strong anti-CIA bias seems to have infused the period after 1966 when the United States became heavily involved in Vietnam. Of some two dozen CIA films, only six or so show "the Company" in a favorable light. Most of the six are so lightly regarded that their favorable depiction is faint praise at best.

1. UNCLE JOE LIVES

In this 1957 thriller, *The Girl in the Kremlin*, Stalin is alive and well and living incognito in sunny Greece, well after his supposed death. Rest assured that they finally kill him off by the end of the film. A gifted Lithuanian lass played by Zsa Zsa Gabor is searching for her twin sister who disappeared at the same time Stalin was supposed to have died. An ex-OSS man played by Lex Barker helps Zsa Zsa as they track Uncle Joe Stalin. They find him in Greece, with a new face and a new name but poor driving skills after years of limo rides. He escapes to die in an auto accident. *Sic semper tyrannis.*

2. THE COMPANY GOES DEEP

At least they should have gone deep with ex-NFL quarterback Joe Namath in this 1979 film named *Avalanche Express*. The CIA man played by Lee Marvin is guarding the life of a Soviet defector on a train ride to freedom. (Joe Namath plays the part of Leroy, a member of Marvin's security team. For this he got fifth billing.) The Soviets do their best to kill the defector (Robert Shaw) but our hero saves the day from all the diabolical schemes including an avalanche. Actually Shaw was not really so lucky. He died of a heart attack while the film was being edited. Less-than-charitable critics suggest that watching this film pushed Shaw over the edge. The film director Mark Robson had also died during filming.

3. *TARGET* (1985)—THE CIA AGENT AS ORDINARY HERO

In *Target* the college dropout son is played by Matt Dillon and his dull respectable businessman father by Gene Hackman. The somewhat disrespectful son has not a clue. Only after Hackman's wife is kidnapped and assassins attempt to kill him does Hackman tell his astonished son that his dull father had been a CIA agent. The convoluted plot ends with the revelation that Hackman's CIA boss is really a Communist double agent who had killed a German agent's wife and children to protect his cover. It is the dead woman's German agent husband who has kidnapped Hackman's wife and been pursuing Hackman in the mistaken belief that Hackman was the culprit. Once blame is properly allotted, the German kills the double agent CIA chief and commits suicide. Not very pretty, but at least ex-agent

Hackman is portrayed as competent, honest, and mentally balanced.

4. AT LAST, A SUPER SPY FOR THE COMPANY

In *The Soldier* (1982), at last we find a super spy flying the American colors. Soviet agents disguised as everyday Palestinian terrorists threaten to blow up the Saudi Arabian oil supply and contaminate it with radioactive plutonium unless Israel pulls out of the West Bank. The desperate U.S. president then calls on the one man who can save the world. Our hero, played by Ken Wahl, deals with the threats of violence in a traditional American way, with violence and bloodshed. The right of Americans to be warm and to drive the vehicles of their choice is preserved and the Israelis stay put.

5. MY FAVORITE—*THREE DAYS OF THE CONDOR* (1975)

This is one of the all-time great adventure flicks. As mentioned elsewhere this started as James Grady's novel, *Six Days of the Condor*, but had to be tightened for the screen. The hero, played by Robert Redford works in a brownstone town house as a reader for a CIA front, The American Literary Historical Society. He spends his days innocently reading comic books and plugging their plots into the CIA computer. In this way, he has unknowingly stumbled onto an active but very secret CIA plot concerning Mideast oil. When he sneaks out the back way for lunch a team of CIA contract assassins kills everyone in the brownstone.

He returns to find everyone dead and spends the next three days, with the help of Faye Dunaway (whom he at first abducts), finding out the truth and evading CIA hit teams sent after him. The ending seems rather lame today, but should probably be seen in the context of the antiwar, anti-CIA, purer-than-thou Vietnam Hollywood that produced it. In his final speech, Mr. Redford gives the CIA a pretty good lambasting. Some of us are just purer than others.

6. *THE BETTER ANGELS* BECOMES *WRONG IS RIGHT*

This movie, *Wrong Is Right* (1982), is based on the novel *The Better Angels* by Charles McCarry. Here the Company takes a sound thrashing, as might be expected in the post-Vietnam, post-Watergate era in which it was produced. The agency is represented as a nest of immoral and amoral screwballs. The CIA is not alone. This satire sticks a knife in several fat targets of the time, from American culture, to television, to political and cultural leaders. Few are spared. The plot has a less than admirable U.S. president authorizing the CIA assassination of a Middle East ruler. The ruler retaliates by threatening to give small nuclear devices to terrorists for demolition in New York and Israel, unless the hapless U.S. president resigns.

7. CLAUDIA LOOKS GREAT, BUT ROCK HUDSON WAS BLINDFOLDED

This satire, slapstick comedy, *Blindfold* (1966) is based on Lucille Fletcher's novel of the same name. As is common in spy flicks the plot is convoluted. Rock Hudson is a psychiatrist hired by the CIA to treat a disturbed scientist the Agency has kidnapped. In the shameless theft category the movie steals the plot device from a 1940s' movie, *Joe Smith, American*. Hudson is blindfolded, as was Smith, but retraces his way to the kidnap victim by remembering the sounds he has heard. Claudia Cardinale is quite fetching in her sweater during the escape scene. Rock Hudson made the women swoon at that time and the men more recently.

8.   A WET KISS GOODNIGHT

As Fidel Castro could testify (the CIA missed him in no fewer that eight tries) one of the CIA's lesser talents is for what the Soviets call "wet jobs," what we might call assassinations. This has not stopped Hollywood from playing on this theme. The movie in question is *The Long Kiss Goodnight* (1996). Our heroine Samantha (Geena Davis) is living as an amnesiac in a nice Norman Rockwell town with her good-looking daughter. Unexpectedly she is attacked and almost murdered; this shock starts to bring her out of her amnesia. Yes, she remembers now, she is a ruthless CIA assassin named Charley. Her first accident had happened because she knew too much and now that her former comrades in arms know she is alive, they are doing their best to see that she has a more successful accident than their efforts one and two. Relax, gentle viewer, Castro is going into a comfortable dotage and so will Samantha/Charley/Geena. The movie is rated R.

9.   THE COMPANY FATHER MAKES THE MOVIES

We will end with two films about the Company's direct ancestor, the World War II Office of Strategic Services (OSS) run by Colonel William Donovan. There is strong feeling that these three were part of Donovan's great publicity campaign to keep the OSS running and promote the cause of a postwar intelligence agency. He was faced with much opposition and pulled out all the stops, to no immediate avail. President Harry Truman dissolved the OSS October 1, 1945, after scarcely 10 day's notice. The favorable treatment Hollywood gave the OSS was not to be continued although the studios and prominent producers had often worked with or for British or American Intelligence during World War II.

The first flick on OSS was released by Paramount in May 1946 and got dibs on the title *OSS*. This is only fitting, since Paramount had been helpful to Donovan's operations. One of its executives, Stanton Griffis, had served as a special OSS agent in Finland. Through him, the studio had supplied the money for OSS operations in Finland and Sweden. The promos for the film said that the lead Alan Ladd "never lived so desperately . . ." and that actress Geraldine Fitzgerald had "never loved so dangerously." This was the only one of the three films to openly advertise its connections to OSS. Half a dozen OSS people are listed in the credits along with a signed statement by Donovan himself. The film was a little too open with classified information for the comfort of the Strategic Services Unit of the War Department (the remainder of OSS), which protested after a private screening. The public did not protest. They liked it, to the tune of $2.8 million in rental fees for the studio, a very respectable take in 1946.

10. *CLOAK AND DAGGER*

The second OSS film was released in October 1946 almost on the first anniversary of OSS's death. The name came from the title of a book by two OSS veterans, Corey Ford and Alastar MacBain. The book was *Cloak and Dagger: The Secret Story of OSS*. In classic Hollywood style the movie had nothing to do with the book except the title. Gregory Peck plays a college professor of physics who becomes an agent in Switzerland to prevent the Nazis from building an atom bomb. Lilli

Palmer, who plays a member of the Italian resistance, provides the romance. There exists no complete copy of this movie as it was scripted. Ring Lardner Jr. and Albert Maltz, the screenwriters, ended the film with a plea against the spread of atomic power (a favorite Soviet theme as the USSR scrambled to build an atom bomb). Warner Brothers removed this ending and destroyed it. A year later, in October 1947 Lardner and Maltz would gain great renown as they were declared in contempt of Congress for failing to answer questions about their ties to the Communist Party. Along with eight other members of the "Hollywood Ten," these two spent a year as guests of the government at a federal penitentiary. *Cloak and Dagger* did well at the box office, earning Warner Brothers $2.5 million.

The Company as Culture Vulture

It was unknown for two decades that the men and women of the CIA were generous patrons of the arts. Literature, music, painting, and the movies all drew the Company's attention and more importantly its money. Of course, this was more than a sensitive concern to uplift the boobs and rubes. This was part of a tough cultural war fought by CIA and British MI-6 against the Soviets from 1950 into the 1980s. The left intelligentsia was, and is, particularly offended by the revelations that have dribbled out since the first *Ramparts* article in 1967.

To understand how the CIA came to cultural awareness in 1950 we must go back into the 1930s and '40s, a period when the intelligentsia and the best universities in Europe and America were hotbeds of leftist thinking, and many intellectuals saw the Soviet Union as the ideal of the future. No city had more leftists per square mile than New York. Indeed, it was said during the 1930s that New York was the most interesting part of the Soviet Union. Soviet Intelligence was able to cultivate hundreds of agents and informants even within the U.S. government. To make the situation worse, the literate American and British publics had been buried in pro-Soviet propaganda during the war. Bamboozling these attentive Americans during World War II had not been hard; unbamboozling them brought cries of anguish.

Today few remember the uproar caused by Winston Churchill's "Iron Curtain Speech," at Fulton, Missouri, in March of 1946. How, asked the literate public, could Churchill say those awful things about Uncle Joe Stalin and our noble Russian allies? Things were much the same in Great Britain. After World War II, the Soviet Union's prestige was great in Europe and 25 percent of the voters in Italy and France voted Communist. The most vociferous, most active intellectuals were very left, often very pro-Communist and in Europe, particularly France, very anti-American. Those who took the mantle of centrists in this bandwagon professed to believe that the Soviet Union and the United States were equally evil.

The CIA's "Congress for Cultural Freedom" was a response not only to these general pro-Communist feelings of many intellectuals but the sponsorship by the Communist Information Bureau (COMINFORM) of a series of cultural conferences. These started in September 1948. They called for world peace and denounced the Truman Doctrine (March 1947) and the Marshall Plan (June 1947). One thing about these CIA-sponsored events and the people subsidized—they were not a very orthodox American crew. That was the CIA's point—to emphasize the great diversity of American and European politics—to contrast them with the rigid orthodoxy of the Communist Bloc. The emphasis here was to back the non-Communist and anti-Communist left in America and Europe, a wild, perhaps even mildly anti-American crew. By the late 1960s, with Vietnam, this group came to be seen as wildly unmanageable. At any rate, here are highlights on the CIA's venture spending tens of millions (hundreds of millions in 2003 dollars) as angel to the arts.

1. NEW YORK—THE BIG APPLE BITES BACK

The Soviets had held the first COMINFORM peace and culture rallies in the sheltered safety of Communist countries where there was a good supply of trained seals, and good comrades knew what happened to bad comrades. The COMINFORM loved it. Next stop, in March 1949—New York City and the Waldorf Astoria Hotel. This is where the Soviet peace bandwagon lost a wheel. Outside, the hotel was ringed by right-wing, often Catholic, pickets; inside was a small, determined band of anti-Soviet intellectuals, often Jews. Soviet cultural stars like the composer Dmitri Shostakovich were trotted out to speak, only to be eaten up by ferocious anti-Communist attacks. Worse, the success of a small band of anti-Communists (often ex-Communists who knew the inside line and tricks) with small funding from the CIA suggested great possibilities to the CIA's Office of Policy Coordination. Might it be possible to push the whole Soviet culture bandwagon into a ditch by funding and promoting those in natural opposition to the Communists? Culture would never be the same.

2. NEXT STOP ON THE CIA'S ROAD TO CULTURE—PARIS

In April in Paris in 1949 the CIA failed to repeat the success of New York. This Soviet-sponsored COMINFORM gathering was a great Communist success. The French were so wildly anti-American and their cultural saints so pro-Stalinist. The writer Jean-Paul Sartre, the existentialist icon, continued to promote the USSR as a guardian of freedom, and his sidekick Jean Genet busied himself denying the existence of the Soviet Gulag of slave labor camps. The American Communist Paul Robeson sang *Old Man River*. The CIA got sick.

3. THE BERLIN BRAIN LIFT

By the summer of 1950 the CIA finally took the bit in its teeth and sponsored a cultural festival just as the Soviets had long been doing. The site was Berlin, Germany. The Berlin airlift of food and supplies had ended but the only real way for people to get into the city was by military aircraft. The ostensible sponsor was, of course, the CIA front, the Congress for Cultural Freedom (CCF), so the money flowed freely and planeloads of American cultural icons made the flight—from playwright Tennessee Williams to *New Leader* editor Sol Levitas to Nobel Prize–winning geneticist Herman Muller. Almost everything went well for the CIA forces. The fates even intervened. Just as the conference opened, the news arrived that Communist forces had invaded South Korea. Ex-Stalinists like Arthur Koestler took the occasion to rabble-rouse the meeting into a crusade and the CIA was really in the Cold Culture War business. The CCF code named Okopera at the CIA became a permanent part of the CIA's Cold War arsenal.

4. THE CIA HOUSE BAND—THE BOSTON SYMPHONY ORCHESTRA

Culture, particularly classical culture, does not come cheap. The Boston Symphony Orchestra (BSO) was widely considered America's best, and the CIA was determined to go at the Communist cultural braggarts head-on. The CIA impresario behind the worldwide junketing of the Boston Symphony was Tom Braden, onetime co-host of CNN's political talk show *Crossfire*. Braden brought all his guns to bear. CIA helper C. D. Jackson, who had taken time from Henry Luce's *Time-Life* to work on Eisenhower's presidential campaign, was a trustee of the BSO. Julius Fleischmann, the yeast and gin man who was the ostensible president of the phony Fairfield Foundation through which the CIA was passing much of the money for the Congress for Cultural Freedom, also stepped in to help. Perhaps the real convincer for the orchestra was a guaranteed grant of $130,000 (around $1 million in 2003 dollars) for 1952. The BSO made its gala debut in Paris in CIA-sponsored "Masterpieces of the Twentieth Century" Festival in April 1952 and did not look back for years. By the time this first tour was done it had set the CIA back $170,000, well over $1 million in 2003 dollars. Very soon nearly all of the music board of the CIA front Congress for Cultural Freedom was in one way or another tied into the music school at Tanglewood, the orchestra's summer home.

5. STUNNING MASTERPIECE

April in Paris again—in 1952 the CIA took its cultural road show to the very heart of culture. It was overpowering. Thirty days of music by nine of the West's greatest orchestras that money could buy, including the Boston Symphony. There were the works of the greatest composers, many of them expressly chosen because they had been banned by Hitler or Stalin or, like Alban Berg, both. Others included Arnold Schoenberg, who had to leave Germany in the early 1930s because his decadent Jewish music irritated Nazis. The same went for Paul Hindemith, Claude Debussy, and Georges Auric.

The art exhibit, put together by John Sweeney, former director of New York's Museum of Modern Art, arrived fittingly on the ship *AA Liberte*. It was a catch-all of modern art, organized on the theme of art that dictators—Hitler and Stalin—hated. At the end, this show went to London's Tate where it also wowed the crowds. The Communist press in France hated the festival and quite rightly identified it as an attempt to enlist the French in the American led anti-Communist cultural army.

6. ABSTRACT EXPRESSIONISM AS A COMPANY PLOT

Remember those right-wing American conservatives who derided Abstract Expressionism—Jackson Pollock and his ilk—as some sort of Commie plot to sap the fiber of red-blooded Americans? Well, they were right—it was a plot, but not by the Communists, who were even more repulsed by Abstract Expressionism than any American know-nothing. (There is fine film footage of Nikita Khrushchev viewing his first Abstract Expressionist art show—he was outraged and had a violent tantrum right there in public.) It was a secret CIA plot put in place both because the Commies hated the stuff and because the American voters would have howled had they known they were supporting such "art" and the weird artists who created it. In fact, they and their Congressmen had howled when the State Department had mounted such a show in the late 1940s. The show had started in Paris and then moved to Eastern Europe where it was a great success, but had to be stopped and the paintings sold for a few cents on the dollar of their cost because of congressional opposition. The Stalinists, of course, did think art should serve the state and they had what they needed—Socialist Realism—all those unreal, overblown heroic figures of men and women with submachine guns or welding torches and plows, building socialism.

The United States has its counterpoint of Capitalist Realism, of course, the unrealistically handsome men and women who sell products in American advertising, but that is another story. For the culture mavens at the CIA, Abstract Expressionism (AE) had several virtues: not only did the Stalinists hate it, but AE made Socialist Realism look even stiffer and more stilted than it really was. Also, it was distinctly American. Its leading practitioner, Jackson Pollock, was a big, boisterous American, born in Wyoming—he took his painting so seriously that he sometimes allowed it to interfere with his drinking problem, sometimes not. Here was an art and artists who were American—free, full of energy, gaudy and big, nay huge (for example, Pollock's "Number 2" is something like 15 feet by 30 feet). The CIA people thought that if America was going to dominate the world, her art should be a major force in that world. The Company had an ace here, Nelson Aldrich Rockefeller, an old intelligence hand. In 1940–1945, Nelson had given two rent-free floors in Rockefeller Center to British Intelligence for their efforts to involve the United States in World War II. He had also worked with British Intelligence and the FBI to keep Nazis out of Latin America in 1940–1941.

In this capacity Rockefeller had been the Coordinator of Inter-American Affairs (CIAA), a British-instigated intelligence organization masquerading as a cultural missionary institute in Latin America. Moreover, his mother had started the Museum of Modern Art (MOMA) and Nelson himself had a vast personal collection of modern art. Joining Rockefeller were two other CIAA friends who had worked for Rockefeller at CIAA: John "Jock" Whitney and William Burden, a Vanderbilt relative. In fact, the MOMA and its directors were tied to intelligence work in such a web of ways that it would take a book to explore them.

On the money front, the Rockefeller Brothers Fund was the donor of record for $125,000 a year (almost a million a year in 2003 dollars) for five years of seed money. The CIA was a determined patron. The single art show in Vienna in 1959 mounted especially to undercut the Communist Youth Festival being held simultaneously cost an additional $35,000 (roughly $250,00 in 2003 dollars), all passed through a variety of fronts. Though the art was a great success and the artists made a pile, many of the real stars did not enjoy it long. Pollock died in a 1956 car crash. Ditto David Smith. Franz Kline lost his bouts with the bottle. Mark Rothko committed suicide, some say in despair at becoming a rich artist by producing art that protested against materialism. He could not face the fact that he was a failure at being a pure, starving artist.

7. THE CIA AND THOSE HIGHBROW MAGAZINES YOUR PROFESSORS READ

The CIA and its organizing and money-dispensing arm, the Congress for Cultural Freedom, backed a whole raft of snooty, and sometimes snotty, highbrow leftist magazines in the 1950s and 1960s. They make such a nice little group of ten they merit their own section (see the next list).

8. THE COMPANY AS BIBLIOPHILE

When the lid blew off this whole cultural caper in the late 1970s the *New York Times* did a story that the CIA had published at least a thousand books. Not all investigators come up with such large numbers, but even by conservative estimates, the CIA was a generous patron. In his book *The Liberal Conspiracy*, Peter Coleman, an editor for the CCF's Australian magazine *Quadrant*, lists some 150 books the Congress for Cultural Freedom published in 15 or more countries. We have already explored a sampling of these.

9. THE COMPANY FOUNDATIONS—FAIRFIELD AND OTHERS

The cash for the Congress for Cultural Freedom's many-pronged attack on the Soviets' cultural fronts, friends, and collaborators was mostly funneled through foundations—the Fairfield Foundation, the J. M. Kaplan Fund, the Gotham Foundation, the Michigan Fund, Andrew Hamilton Fund, Bordon Fund, Price Fund, Beacon Fund, Edsel Fund, and the Kentifield Fund are good examples. Many of the cooperating funds were totally phony, created out of whole CIA cloth, but other real and legitimate funds were acting out of patriotic duty. The lid came off this arrangement in August 1964 just as the United States started overtly bombing North Vietnam.

Congressman Wright Patman of the House Ways and Means Committee had been told in confidence that the J. M. Kaplan Fund, one of those tax-exempt foundations he was investigating, was really a money-laundering scheme for the CIA. In a classic congressional maneuver, Patman leaked this information to the press and the lid was off. The liberal press heaped praise on the Congressman and abuse on the CIA. *The Nation* wrote, "Rep. Wright Patman is to be commended for his decision to disclose, even though he had apparently been told it in confidence . . ." and continued, ". . . this is a typically clumsy CIA maneuver which has only the appearance of cleverness."

This opening allowed the *New York Times* to use these foundation tax forms in 1966 to trace the money for a series of articles exposing the Congress for Cultural Freedom. However, these people were not on the inside. The real *coup de grace* came when the CIA man who had run part of this, Tom Braden, did a tell-all article for the May 20, 1967, edition of *The Saturday Evening Post,* aggressively titled "I Am Glad the CIA is Immoral." By 1967, the Non-Communist Left (NCL) that the CIA had funded to fight Communism had become anti-American and was actively trying to thwart U.S. efforts against the Communist regime in North Vietnam. Some think Braden's revelations were a good way to get rid of ties to the left that were now counterproductive. The non-Communist left was now an enemy; it was time the CIA stopped paying to get beat up.

10. THE VOICE OF THE CIA—PROPRIETARIES OF nEWS InFORMATIOn AnD CULTURE

The Brits always sold British culture with the BBC's World Service. The Soviets sent Radio Moscow to do battle with the West. In fact, Radio Moscow shortwave presented a nice tight English news show during my college days. The CIA got into this in the 1950s in a major way with two "proprietaries," radio companies that it owned—Radio Free Europe (RFE) and Radio

Liberty (RL). They were free only in the sense that CIA management was loose and the announcers, often staunch anti-Communist refugees from Eastern Europe, frequently said what they pleased. Nothing has really changed. The U.S. government still pays the freight for RFE and RL. After the CIA's cover was blown the State Department fed them openly.

Encounter et al., the CIA's Stable of Highbrow Culture Magazines

M uch of the generosity to the arts was targeted at the highest levels of the intelligentsia—the trend-setters who, the thought was, would then write the books, teach the students, and spread the ideas—a sort of intellectual trickle-down theory. Therefore, this project was counted a big triumph even though the most successful of these journals never had a circulation of 35,000 and many were in the 3,000 to 5,000 circulation range. That counts the thousands of free subscriptions also paid for by the CIA. (The operative phrase was that the CIA front would "guarantee" the circulation.) Not many would pay real money to read this stuff.

Once taken off financial life support they went belly up. One of the prime CIA targets was the fuzzy-headed English publication the *New Statesman and Nation* (NSN), which was thought to be carrying water for the Soviet Union. Even more galling, the *NSN* had, by literary standards, a huge circulation of 85,000. Things had

been very tough for the *NSN* rivals; four of them—
Horizon, Penguin New Writing, Cambridge Journal,
and *Scrutiny*—had gone bust between 1950 and 1953.
So the CIA and British Intelligence were searching to
build a literary rival with friendlier views. They tried one
called *The Twentieth Century* but that did not work out.
However, as is common in the real world, time and
money eventually had their day and the CIA played
fairy moneymother to a worldwide chain of leftist intellectual magazines. And they were very leftist. When the
editor of the Austrian part of this enterprise called
Forum reprinted an article from William F. Buckley's
conservative American magazine *National Review*, he
was toughly reprimanded by the head of the CIA front
Congress for Cultural Freedom: "It is beneath the dig-
nity of a Congress journal to reprint something from the
completely discredited *National Review*." Capitalism,
particularly American capitalism, was totally disdained
by European intellectuals after the war, and any hint of
belief in such nonsense would completely discredit the
speaker.

1. *ENCOUNTER* (1953–1990)

The flagship of this fleet was *Encounter*, produced in
London. *Newsweek* wrote that *Encounter* is "as open-
minded, as animated, and as brilliantly bitchy, as a
successful literary cocktail party." The first issue came
out in October 1953 with a wide collection of entries,
from Virginia Woolf's diaries and some poetry to a
tough political article on the Rosenberg atom spies and
an equally tough review of Isaac Deutscher's *Russia
after Stalin*. The Stalinists and their fellow travelers did
not like it and said so in reviews, but the first modest
printing of 10,000 sold out in a week.

The hard anti-Stalinist hooks were well buried in the intellectual bait. The offerings were relentlessly highbrow, great fun for the literati and often, as mentioned, "bitchy." Jessica Mitford threw spears at everyone in "The English Aristocracy"; John Sparrow's "Regina v Penguin" covered sodomy in *Lady Chatterley's Lover;* Wayland Young discussed the lives of London prostitutes in "Sitting on a Fortune."

This was very imaginative cultural warfare against the staid Soviets, but one must be inspired indeed to think of the U.S. Congress of the 1950s knowingly paying for this stuff. However, there was more for Congressmen to chew on had they known that both editors, Irving Kristol and Stephen Spender, had been Communists in the 1930s—Kristol a Trotskyite and Spender a Stalinist noted for his romantic homosexual poetry. *Encounter*'s circulation climbed to 35,000, a great figure for a magazine of its type, but unfortunately only half the circulation needed to be a real capitalist example of profit making. There were a dozen more such journals of culture and opinion, all in one way or another on the CIA tab.

2. *LES PREUVES* IS IN THE PUDDING

The objective in France was to create a competitor for the pro-Soviet Jean-Paul Sartre and his influential literary vehicle, *Les Temps Modernes.* The Communists had a strong political and cultural hold in France, almost as strong a hold as the anti-Americanism, pacifism, and neutralism that seemed to suffuse the Left Bank intellectuals. This project was a major challenge. No Frenchman of sufficient literary reputation would even take the editor's job. The CCF had to hire another ex-Communist, Francois Bondy from Switzerland.

The first issue of *Preuves*, which translates as "proof," came out in October 1951. The French responded with what today's politically correct Americans might call hate speech. It sounded better in French, of course. But the French did not leave it at just talk. An issue was confiscated in 1958 and finally in 1962 the Paris offices of the Congress for Cultural Freedom was bombed. These last two events were in direct response to *Preuves*'s editorial stand on the Algerian Crisis, which brought de Gaulle back into power. The high point for *Preuves* came in late 1956 and 1957, as it did for many anti-Stalinist, CIA-funded magazines. In November 1956, a revolt failed in Hungary, put down by the Soviets with tanks and considerable bloodshed. This was hard on neutralists and pacifists. In that year Nikita Khruschev had delivered a secret speech to the Communist Party faithful, telling them what all but the comatose already knew—that Joseph Stalin was a pretty awful person. The CIA and the Israeli Mossad found a party member who wished to become seriously involved with capitalism and who had a copy of Mr. Khrushchev's musings. When the money cleared, the CIA had the speech, which it published to the deep embarrassment of Stalin lovers everywhere, not excluding France. The circulation was never higher than 3,000 per year, but everybody congratulated himself and called this a great achievement in France. It really helps to have low expectations.

3. DOES *CUADERNOS* MEAN DEAD ON ARRIVAL IN SPANISH?

The Congress started *Cuadernos* in 1953. *Cuadernos* was published in Paris in Spanish and was intended for the Latin audience in the Western Hemisphere. It was

edited by ex-Communist Julian Gorkin, whose real sur-
name was Gomaz. Despite heavy infusions of cash and
a large free list, it was hard to get anyone in Latin
America to read *Cuadernos*. Even the Congress for
Cultural Freedom's ploy of sending American cultural
stars to visit Latin America went awry. On a 1962 tour
of Brazil, Argentina, and Paraguay to give some
speeches, attend parties, and generally show himself,
the highly acclaimed American poet Robert Lowell
gave a performance few in Buenos Aires will forget. He
threw away his anti-mania drugs, substituting large
numbers of martinis. Thus primed, he enlightened his
listeners on the positive aspects of Hitler's political phi-
losophy, declared himself to be the "Caesar of Argentina," then took off his clothes so as to better mount the
various equestrian statues that presented themselves
in the city. It took six paramedics to get him into a
straitjacket and several thousand milligrams of Thora-
zine to get him ready to ship back to the States. Even
strapped down, the irrepressible Lowell enticed Keith
Botsford from the CCF or CIA to whistle "Yankee Doo-
dle Dandy" or the "Battle Hymn of the Republic."
Whether he succeeded at his original mission to take
the Latins' attention off Communist intellectuals like
Pablo Neruda is open to question, but he did arm-
wrestle the exiled left-wing Spanish poet on the floor at
a party. Those Americans make such a cultural splash.

The late 1950s and early 1960s brought joy to Latin
American Communists and their North American-
hating amigos. Fidel took over Cuba and everything
seemed to be going their way. The sight of boatlifts and
thousands of ordinary people trying to escape Fidel's
poverty-stricken workers' paradise was years in the
future. The only way *Cuadernos* could have gained

respect would have been to launch a virulent anti-American campaign, which seemed to be going a little too far. *Cuadernos* was officially laid to rest in 1965. Despite vast amounts of money, at least $300,000 (2001 dollars), in some years it was barely alive. It had been impossible to recruit young Latin intellectuals to write for it. A replacement left-wing magazine, *Mundo Nuevo*, was started in 1966. It quickly attracted great young writing talents. Its credo, *Fidelismo sin Fidel*, Fidelism without Fidel seemed to have possibilities for attracting the Latin intelligentsia, but by then the CIA's funding of the Congress was starting to leak and *Mundo* was put to sleep in 1971.

4. *SOVIET SURVEY*

The *Survey* began in 1955 as a four-page mimeographed monthly and quickly grew to a large quarterly. It had no competition; it filled a void. No one in the West was covering Soviet artistic and scientific life. Walter Laqueur, a German Jew who had gone to Israel in 1938, edited it. This was a first-rate magazine, largely written by Laqueur under the name Mark Alexander, and it did a first-rate job of covering events in a largely closed Soviet society. It sometimes did too good a job for its own peace of mind. The editors were thrown into a tizzy when Soviet publications started quoting material from *Survey*, as it had been renamed.

5. A NON-NEUTRAL FOR AUSTRIA

This journal *Forum* took its first breath in 1954. It was yet another voice echoing the themes from the mother ship, the Congress for Cultural Freedom. *Forum* drummed on the end of ideology and vigorously attacked neutralism and neutrals. The talented editor was Friedrich Torberg (1908–1979), a humorist, poet, and critic. He was "Freddy the Tort," to those who thought they knew him. Like many who thrive in this twilight world, he had undergone several transmogrifications and like many others went by a name other than that of his birth; born in Vienna as Kantor-Berg he had ended up in New York. The Communists immediately attacked the "Tort" and *Forum* as American agents (smart people, those Communists) and tools. He and *Forum* survived this to become a major force in Austria. It was most valuable during the failed Hungarian Revolution of November 1956. As the refugees flooded across the border into Austria, *Forum* was the perfect visible vehicle to provide money, advice, and quick language training for fleeing intellectuals. *Forum's* performance was so impressive that in 1958 the Austrian government bestowed on the modestly schooled Torberg the title Professor.

6. *DER MOnaT*—THE OTHER GERMAN TOOL

Der Monat is the only one of these magazines that started life as a visible tool of the United States. It had been created in the late 1940s by HICOG, the High Commission of Germany. It was a first-class journal, with big-name intellectual writers. On the left, the visible ownership left it vulnerable to criticism by anti-Americans and the Communists. On the right, the knives were out because of *Der Monat's* persistent leftist slant and its equally persistent antireligious slant. Both of these were simply basic, fundamental beliefs of European intellectuals of the period. Despite leftist cries for an open forum of ideas, the reality was that no journal that espoused capitalism or failed to bash Christian churches would get a hearing.

Accordingly, the editor Melvin Lasky published big-name activist religion bashers like Bertrand Russell. This brought on attacks by the hierarchy of the U.S. Catholic Church. Rather than using visible dollars from U.S. taxpayers, the visible costs were taken over by the more open-minded Ford Foundation starting in 1954. The editors made a big, public, utterly fraudulent profession of independence as *Der Monat* moved firmly into the CIA stable of Congress publications. It published American writers—Norman Mailer, William Faulkner—and German writers and extracts from anti-Stalinist books like Milovan Djillis's *The New Class*. When the Congress for Cultural Freedom hosted guests in Berlin for example, the actor Gary Cooper and the writer Thornton Wilder, the staff of *Der Monat* actually did the honors. By 1958 when Melvin Lasky transferred to London to run *Encounter*, he had built *Der Monat's* circulation to 25,000.

7. *QUADRANT*, THE RED BASHER FROM DOWN UNDER

Though this looks like a native Australian growth, *Quadrant's* real origins are reputed to have been in the Russian Tea Room in New York City. The purpose, as usual, was to counter the great influence of Communists, pinkos, and fellow travelers in the cultural and scientific life of Australia. The man chosen to edit *Quadrant* was James McAuley, at that time a conservative Roman Catholic, but once again a man with a twisted ideological past. The first issue was published just after the November 1956 Russian invasion of Hungary. The brutal suppression of this revolution put the left and its peace rhetoric and philo-Sovietism on the defensive, and *Quadrant* tried to keep them there.

Quadrant was the most conservative of the Congress publications and the only one still publishing.

8. nOT FOR THE ARTSY-CRAFTSY—*SCIEnCE anD FREEDOM*

The Congress for Cultural Freedom had a Committee on Science and Freedom that sponsored a conference on this subject at Hamburg, Germany, in 1953. The basic theme was that the scientific community should be self-governing, which it obviously was not in Communist countries. This, of course, follows the basic CIA/MI-6 theme of creating as many hassles as possible for the Soviets on any issue where Soviet practices differed from theoretical purity. Intellectuals were thought to be vulnerable here. In this vein, it also campaigned against apartheid in South Africa and for academic freedom everywhere.

Science and Freedom (S&F) had short, lively articles and was highly controversial in the 1950s. In 1961, it was thought that *S&F* had outlived its usefulness. It was dropped, and the Congress for Cultural Freedom put forth a new academically targeted journal named *Minerva* in 1962. Where *Science and Freedom* had had a mailing list of 5,000–6,000 (not quite a paid subscription list, but close enough for CIA work), *Minerva* never made it above 2,000. It presented very high-toned stuff for only the most high-toned in academia.

9. *JIYU* (MEANS "FREEDOM" In JAPAnESE)

Japan was a tough sell for the Congress. The anti-Americanism and pro-Communism among Japanese intellectuals set new benchmarks. The Soviet launch of Sputnik in October 1957 had largely made up for the Communist PR disasters in suppressing rebellions in Poland and Hungary in the previous year. Anti-American riots in 1960 were so bad that President Eisenhower canceled his goodwill visit to Japan. There was an early false start when the CIA found the first version of *Jiyu* to have the sort of truly independent editor that the public relations pronouncements said it had.

Obviously this would not do, so the Congress (called the Japanese Cultural Forum in Japan) tried again and succeeded. For around a quarter of a million 2003 dollars, the CIA had a correct magazine of slightly under 6,000 circulation. Things went fine. The August 1964 leak, by Congressman Wright Patman, exposing the CIA funding of the Congress for Cultural Freedom caused few problems, but Tom Braden's "I'm Glad the CIA is Immoral," brought the house down, literally, in Japan. The editor had his house burned and he needed police protection.

10. TRANSITION TO NOWHERE

The last of these CIA-sponsored assaults on the world's pulpwood supply that we will explore was called *Transition: A Journal of the Arts, Culture and Society*. It was published in Uganda. It seems to have started out as a worthy, independent magazine in late 1961, but, as one might expect from its title, did not have mass appeal and soon ran out of money. Then the pure, but poor, publisher Rajat Neogy appealed to the Congress for Cultural Freedom's African agent for money. No problem, said the agent and thus was born a lively six-year relationship. *Transition* published the best African writers mixed with the Congress's usual collection of leftist European intellectuals. Its circulation reached an amazing 12,000, including 3,000 subscribers in the United States. Unfortunately the writers were uncompromisingly pure and the Ugandan dictator equally so. When the CCF's CIA affiliation was bandied about in 1967 and 1968 the Ugandan police raided *Transition*'s offices and jailed its top editors, including Neogy. They wrote some wonderful "when I get out of jail letters" about their dedication to liberal ideals.

Ten Selected Books Published by the CIA Front Congress for Cultural Freedom

The Congress for Cultural Freedom (CCF) published dozens of books in at least 15 countries. Most of them are the sort of academic sandbags read by only a few specialists. Following standard academic procedure the Congress would invite a list of notables to a conference, pay all their expenses, and invite them to deliver papers. The papers would then be collected and published as a book, often with chapters whose only common thread was their binding. Try these CCF titles: *Problems of Maharashtra* (report of Bombay Seminar, May 1960); *Music—East and West* (conference reports on 1961 Tokyo East-West Music Encounter); *Tradition and Change in Sudanese Society* (report of the Khartoum Seminar, January 1961). Obviously some angel would have to pay to get such stirring titles into print. The CIA was that angel to the academic and cultural community. Below are 10 titles chosen because they had some commercial possibilities of their own. The

CIA front just gave them an extra push. For a more complete list see Peter Coleman, *The Liberal Conspiracy*, a history of the Congress for Cultural Freedom.

1. HONEY, P. J. *NORTH VIETNAM TODAY: PROFILE OF A COMMUNIST SATELLITE*. NEW YORK: FREDERICK PRAEGER, 1962.

Praeger was a favorite CIA publisher who put out two dozen or so titles at the Agency's behest. He was either paid directly, or the Agency simply guaranteed the sale of enough books to make the deal financially attractive. Needless to say, this is also a great way to get on the best-seller list.

2. LAQUEUR, WALTER, AND LEOPOLD LABEDZ. *THE FUTURE OF COMMUNIST SOCIETY*. NEW YORK: PRAEGER, 1962.

Laqueur and Labedz were the editors of the Congress for Cultural Freedom's periodical, first called *Soviet Survey* and then simply *Survey* because the authorities in the Mideast did not like anything with the name "Soviet."

3. HUDSON, G. F., RICHARD LOWENTHAL, AND RODERICK MACFARQUHAR. *THE SINO-SOVIET DISPUTE*. NEW YORK: PRAEGER, 1961.

Hudson was an Oxford historian who frequently worked the circuit of CCF conferences and even helped host them. It is hard to think of anyone besides an intelligence agency or a deep-pockets moneybags who would pay for these extensive translations and commentaries.

4. **RORTY, JAMES, AND MOSHE DECTER. *MCCARTHY AND THE COMMUNISTS*. BOSTON: BEACON PRESS, 1954.**

This was one of the first books to attempt an evaluation of Senator Joseph McCarthy as a fighter against Communism.

5. **SCALAPINO, ROBERT A. *NORTH KOREA TODAY*. NEW YORK AND LONDON: FREDERICK A. PRAEGER, 1963.**

These nine articles were first published in *China Quarterly* and cover the social, political, and economic goings-on in North Korea. Nobody else was showing North Korea in a bad light, so the CIA did it.

6. **BLAKE, PATRICIA, AND MAX HAYWARD (EDS.). *HALF-WAY TO THE MOON: NEW WRITING FROM RUSSIA*. LONDON: WEIDENFELD & NICOLSON, 1964.**

This collection first appeared in *Encounter*. The themes vary widely but all emphasize individual ideas outside the individual and his ideas outside Communist ideology. Alexander Solzhenitsyn is particularly pointed in this regard with a piece titled "Matryona's Home."

7. **LASKY, MELVIN J. (ED.). *THE HUNGARIAN REVOLUTION*. INTRO. BY HUGH SETON-WATSON. LONDON: SECKER & WARBURG, 1957.**

The Soviet crushing of the 1956 Hungarian Revolution created a crisis among non-Communist bloc intellectuals and this volume, printed in several languages, made sure that the facts and their proper interpretation were widely distributed. The introduction to the French edition was by Raymond Aaron.

8. **DRAPER, THEODORE.** *CASTRO'S REVOLUTION: MYTHS AND REALITIES.* **TOKYO: RONSO-SHA, 1963 (ORIGINALLY PUBLISHED IN NEW YORK: PRAEGER, 1962).**

9. **SORENSON, THEODORE C.** *DECISION-MAKING IN THE WHITE HOUSE.* **TOKYO: JIYU-SHA, 1964 (ORIGINALLY PUBLISHED IN NEW YORK AND LONDON: COLUMBIA UNIVERSITY PRESS, 1963).**

10. **T.S. ELIOT.** *FOUR QUARTETS,* **IN RUSSIAN.**

The word is that the CIA commissioned this translation and had the volumes air-dropped behind the Iron Curtain.

It Always Sounds Better in French— Especially If You Don't Know French

In the 17th and 18th centuries when the interrelated modern ideas of the state, warfare, diplomacy, romance, and spying were taking shape, France was at the very epicenter of such doings. Setting the style was the French "Sun" King, Louis XIV (reigned 1643–1715). And such a style it was; his stunning palace at Versailles, a dozen or so miles southwest of Paris, was so impressive that envious rulers scattered dozens of scaled-down copies across the Continent. In espionage, Louis XIV is fully recognizable to the modern reader. As one commentator, Saint-Simon, later wrote of the diligent king: "Louis XIV took great pains to inform himself on what was happening everywhere, in public places, private homes, and even on the international scene. . . . Spies and informers of all kinds were numberless. . . . [His most] vicious method of securing information was opening letters."

But back to the French language—the other rulers of Europe were so impressed with *la toute Francaise*

(TOOT FRAHN SAYZ) that French became the language of diplomacy. Soon it became the royal court language of Sweden, Poland, Germany, and even Russia. Since then the French have been experts at warfare, diplomacy, sex, and espionage for so long they always have exactly the correct word or phrase for anything you might have thought of doing, no matter how strange, disgusting or kinky. The bitter British-French rivalry of the 14th through 19th centuries was only smoothed over at the turn of the 20th century and is still evident in the language: The French always sound so elegant and romantic no matter what one is saying. Take the word "Espionage" itself—it sounds so much better and more refined than "Spying." Some of this French is so precise, correct, and useful that it has become part of English. For example: *Coup d'etat* (KOO DAY TAH) has become so familiar even English journalists habitually say, "There was a *Coup* (KOO) in country X last night." Let us examine a few French phrases: Diplomacy—*Tour d'horizon* (TOUR DUH OAR-I-ZON). The French term sounds magnificent and exciting. In actuality it describes a general diplomatic bull session where either nothing specific was on the agenda or no one wanted to talk about the agenda. On making love—*Elle est une sacree baiseuse* (EL A OON SAH-KREH BAY-ZOOS). In French this enticing phrase seems to convey a blessed sense of wonder and amazement. Perhaps God himself has sent an angel. To my ears the English—She is a hell of a good f---,—sounds entirely too rough and lacks a proper sense of appreciation.

1. **On DISLOYALTY**

Traison (TRAY-ZON): This is just your good old garden variety political treason for which so many have been hanged, or shot, or drawn and quartered or whatever treatment was fashionable in their age. See how this nasty idea is smoothed over by saying it in French. This word is so fundamental to espionage, since one is always either committing treason or trying to get someone else to do so.

2. REFOULEMENT (RUH-FOOL-MAHN)

Here is a less known but still striking example. No matter how heartless the activity, it always seems like the very foundation of sweetness and light in French. *Refoulement* means the deliberate forcing back of persons seeking sanctuary as refugees. Turning a blind eye and a cold shoulder to desperate displaced persons requires an iron stomach. See what a help a fancy French word can be.

3. RAISON D'ETAT (RAY-ZONE DAY-TAH)

Espionage and covert operations can be a tough business and often there is little in the law of one's country to sanction black bag jobs, or political assassinations. *Raison d'etat* means "reason of state," the safety and security interests of, for example, 285 million U.S. citizens that take precedence over private morality. If eliminating Osama bin Laden will enhance the safety and sense of security of these citizens, then *raison d'etat* is the reasonable sounding phrase that explains the uncivil, unthinkable, or unreasonable sounding action.

4. ECOUTES SAUVAGE (A-KOOT SO-VAHJ)

Ecoutes sauvage actually means unauthorized telephone tap in France. French politics are so quaint and imaginative. There is an outfit called the *Commission Nationale de Controle des Interceptions de Securité,* which is supposed to oversee wire taps, but what with political "cohabitation" (the president and the prime minister are of different parties) everyone naturally eavesdrops on everyone else in a regular free-for-all. Many retired intelligence men run private "information" services on a freelance basis. The taps authorized by the Elysee Palace alone (the president's office) are said to number over a thousand politicians, journalists, and even an actress, Carole Bouquet.

5. "FILE À TON TRAVAIL, ESPION" (FEEL AH TONE TRAH-VEYE, ES-P-OWN)

This, if you do not recognize it, is that indefatigable cheerleader for the British Empire, Rudyard Kipling, in *The Spy's March* (1913). This is the French rendering of "Get to your business, spy." Actually, Kipling's original demands a drum roll before this line.

6. AGENCE CENTRAL DE RENSEIGNEMENTS (AH-JAHNCE CEN-TRAHL DUH RAY-SEINE-MAHN)

Maybe we should have used this romantic-sounding name for the Central Intelligence Agency (CIA) during the 1970s and '80s when the American intellectual class was so down on the Agency.

7. MORT AUX ESPIONS (MORE OH ES PEE OWN)

As you can see, French even dresses up an outfit like SMERSH, the Soviet-era assassination outfit with the motto you see here, "Death to Spies."

8. MICRO-EMETTEUR MINIATURISE SAISI SUR UN AGENT FEMININ (BOUCLES D'OREILLES). (MICRO EMIT UR MINI AH TURE EAZE SIGH SEE SEWER OON AH-JAHNT FEM EE NIN BOO-KLAY DOOR EEL

Suppose you are with an enticing mademoiselle in the cozy little club off the Champs Elysees. You pull her close and whisper in her ear. "Ma Cherie. . . ." Meanwhile, Pierre, in the back room is frantically turning the dials to keep from having his ears and his sensitive receiving equipment blown out. The French phrase above is the more charming way of saying "miniature radio transmitter," which is concealed in a woman agent's earrings. There is also a companion brooch for mademoiselle's bosom that works the same way. One would hope that since you are a gentleman Pierre's eardrums would be a little safer.

q. *PAR L'ASSASSINAT ET L'ENLEVEMENT* (PAR LAS-A-SIN-A EH LEN LEH VAY MAH)

This is the hard stuff. The above is French for assassination. And of course, the French should say this well for they have done so many of them. Remember Peter Wright of Britain's MI-5 deflecting CIA's James Angleton's request for help with an assassination: "Have you tried the French? This is more their kind of thing."—and so it is. Embarrassingly, these have come to the public's attention. Even if, as in the case of sinking Greenpeace's *Rainbow Warrior,* French Intelligence meant only to sink the boat and not to kill anyone.

10. *AGENT PROVOCATEUR* (AH JAHNT PRO VAH KA TOUR)

An *agent provocateur* is a secret agent sent by the intelligence agency to infiltrate groups and incite them to premature acts that will tie up their leaders in court proceedings or jail time, or turn public opinion against them. There are some fuzzy areas here, as in much of espionage. *Par example:* In 1970 an FBI agent infiltrated an American anti-Vietnam War group that wished to break into a draft board office. Since the members of the group were idealistic and enthusiastic but ignorant college students, the agent had to train them. As he later told the U.S. Senate's Church Committee: "Everything they learned about breaking into a building or climbing a wall or cutting glass or destroying lockers, I taught them . . . and the FBI supplied me with the equipment needed."

Bibliography

Adkins, Paul. *Codeword Dictionary: A Compilation of Military and Law Enforcement Codewords from 1904 to Present.* Osceola, WI: Motorbooks, 1997.

Becket, Henry S.A. (pseud.). *The Dictionary of Espionage: Spookspeak into English.* New York: Stein and Day, 1986.

Berkeley, Roy. *A Spy's London.* London: Leo Cooper, 1994.

Brown, Anthony Cave. *"C" The Secret Life of Sir Stewart Menzies, Spymaster to Winston Churchill.* New York, Macmillan Publishing Co., 1987.

Buitrago, Ann Mari, and Leon Andrew Immerman. *Are You Now or Have You Ever Been in the FBI Files?* New York: Grove Press, 1981.

Buranelli, Vincent and Nan Buranelli. *Spy/Counterspy: An Encyclopedia of Espionage.* New York: McGraw-Hill, 1982.

Carl, Leo D. *The International Dictionary of Intelligence and Counterintelligence.* McLean, VA: International Defense Consultant Services, Inc, 1990.

Chadwin, Mark Lincoln. *The Hawks of World War II.* Chapel Hill: The University of North Carolina Press, 1968.

Coleman, Peter. *The Liberal Conspiracy: The Congress for Cultural Freedom and the Struggle for the Mind of Postwar Europe.* New York: The Free Press, 1989.

Dobson, Christopher, and Ronald Payne. *The Dictionary of Espionage.* London: Harrap, 1984.

Dunlop, Richard. *Donovan: America's Master Spy.* Chicago: Rand McNally, 1982.

Freeman, Charles W. *The Diplomat's Dictionary (rev. ed.).* Washington, D.C.: United States Institute of Peace, 1997.

Frolik, Josef. *The Frolik Defection: The Memoirs of an Intelligence Agent.* London: Leo Cooper, 1975.

Godson, Roy. *Dirty Tricks or Trump Cards: U.S. Covert Action and Counterintelligence.* Dulles, VA: Brassey's, 1995.

Kessler, Pamela. *Undercover Washington: Touring the Sites Where Famous Spies Lived, Worked, and Loved.* McLean, VA: EPM Publications, 1992.

Kessler, Ronald. *Spy vs. Spy: The Shocking True Story of the FBI's Secret War Against Soviet Agents in America.* New York: Pocket Books, 1988.

Knightly, Phillip, and Caroline Kennedy. *An Affair of State: The Profumo Case and the Framing of Stephen Ward.* New York: Atheneum, 1987.

Lashmar, Paul, and James Oliver. *Britain's Secret Propaganda War, 1948–1977.* United Kingdom: Sutton Publishing, 1998.

Mahl, Thomas E. *Desperate Deception: British Covert Operations in the United States, 1939–1944.* Dulles, VA: Brassey's, 1998.

Masters, Anthony. *Literary Agents: The Novelist as Spy.* New York: Basil Blackwell, 1987.

Melton, H. Keith, and Oleg Kalugin. *The Ultimate Spy Book*. London: Dorling Kindersley, 1996.

O'Toole, G. J. A. *Honorable Treachery: A History of U.S. Intelligence, Espionage, and Covert Action from the American Revolution to the CIA*. New York: The Atlantic Monthly Press, 1991.

Polmar, Norman, and Thomas B. Allen. *The Encyclopedia of Espionage*. New York: Gramercy Books, 1997.

Porch, Douglas. *The French Secret Service*. New York: Farrar, Straus and Giroux, 1995.

Roberstein, Herbert, and Eric Breindel. *The Venona Secrets*. Washington, D.C.: Regnery Publishing Co., 2000.

Saunders, Frances Stonor. *The CIA and the World of Arts and Letters: The Cultural Cold War*. New York: New Press, 1999.

Seth, Ronald. *Encyclopedia of Espionage*. London: Book Club Associates, 1974.

Thomas, Gordon. *Gidion's Spies: The Secret History of the Mossad*. New York: St. Martin's Press, 1999.

Troy, Thomas F. *Wartime Washington: The Secret OSS Journal of James Grafton Rogers, 1942–1943*. Frederick, MD: University Publications of America, 1987.

West, Nigel (ed.). *The Faber Book of Espionage*. London: Faber and Faber, 1993.

Winks, Robin. *Cloak and Gown: Scholars in the Secret War, 1939–1961*. New York: William Morrow, 1987.

Wolf, Markus. *Man Without a Face*. New York: Random House, 1997.

Wright, Peter, with Paul Greengrass. *Spy Catcher: The Candid Autobiography of a Senior Intelligence Officer*. New York: Viking, 1987.

Index